MEHER BABA'S
SAMADHI

TALES *from* THE BELOVED'S Tomb

COMPILED AND EDITED BY
IRMA SHEPPARD

242 pp.
Hoefler Text font
1 2 3 4 5 6 7 8 9 0

Published 2020
Asheville, NC USA

ISBN 978-0-578-76040-7

AMB Publishing resides in the hearts of Mankind

Table of Contents

Dedication

Dedicated to the Love we experience in our hearts
as He makes Himself known to us in
His countless unfathomable ways.

Acknowledgements

It has been my privilege to collect these many stories of Baba lovers' experiences in and near Baba's Samadhi. Baba must enjoy variety, for He has given us these diverse experiences for His own reasons. Some stories are uplifting and heartwarming. Some challenge our limited understanding and facilitate growth. Some are humorous, to be enjoyed...simply to be enjoyed. I am grateful to each person who has shared a story for this collection. I am also grateful to all those who sent their artwork and photographs to be included in this book. I trust we all benefit from reading these tales.

Irma Sheppard, August 2020
Asheville, North Carolina

Introduction

In December of 2018 I offered a Baba meeting at my house in Weaverville, North Carolina, called "Tales from the Crypt." Because we seem to gravitate toward our more serious memories, I asked people to bring lighter stories about their experiences in and around the Samadhi. We heard some truly wonderful tales, many funny, all sweet.

The meeting was such a hit that Karl [Moeller, layout and design] and Irma decided to collect our stories for a book, but they wanted to use the serious ones as well as those that made us laugh.

When Irma put out a call for submissions, however, a few people felt that the title was disrespectful and we realized that *Tales from the Crypt* would not do for the cover of a book. The title went through several incarnations before being reborn as *Meher Baba's Samadhi: Tales from The Beloved's Tomb*

For me, the process was a lesson of non-attachment: I loved the original name, and after all, Baba's Tomb-shrine was first called the crypt. I certainly meant no disrespect, and in any case, Baba did have a God-sized sense of humor. But I defer to perhaps wiser minds than my own. *Meher Baba's Samadhi: Tales from The Beloved's Tomb* it is.

Please accept our always heart-opening, occasionally heart-rending, sometimes even humorous offering of stories. May they transport you back to Meherabad, under the highway and railroad tracks, up the Hill, and all the way to Meher Baba's feet.

Susan McKendree, April 2020

Samadhi

by Jimmy Khan

The first time I saw and entered Meher Baba's Samadhi was on February 1, 1969, when Beloved Baba's body was in the crypt. On February 7th His body was covered, for all time to come, with a wooden box—sufficient earth was spread over that to also cover the steps leading to the surface. From day one, Mansari (Mani Desai from Navsari) was in charge of the Samadhi. She would open the Samadhi doors at 5.30 in the morning. We would do morning and evening artis at 7 inside the Samadhi—six of us would stand on the side platforms, three on each side. During the day we could sit on the side platforms in the Samadhi as well.

After about six months, one morning Mansari opened the doors and to her horror saw the earth level in the crypt area had sunk 6 inches. This was far from a miracle of any sort. According to me, the wooden box that covered Baba's body had collapsed with time and hence the earth sank.

The platform and the men mandalis' meditation cabins, which adjoined the Samadhi next to Baba's Cabin were the first to be dismantled. In the early days we could climb up the water tower and have a bird's eye view of the Samadhi—the only place to be able to see that. No more.

After some time Rano Gailey went to Italy, spending her own money to select a marble slab, get it polished and etched with golden lettering. The marble slab arrived and Padri kaka threw a tantrum, saying that there were pink veins in the marble. The mandali pacified him and the slab was installed with sheer muscle power in the small confines of the Samadhi.

From time to time the women mandali came from Meherazad. First they would enter the East Room, then they would go inside the Samadhi, close the doors and sit for a while. A small group of women would follow and surrounded them from the East Room to the Samadhi and back, some holding umbrellas to shade the women mandali. During Amartithi the women mandali went inside the Samadhi just before the 15 minutes of Silence and sat for a while.

In the early days there was no permanent roofing outside the Samadhi as we see today. Maybe a temporary shed was put up. These benches came much later. But there were benches nevertheless to sit on. We did our evening arti with lanterns as there was no electricity then. For years on end there were no flowers at Meherabad. You had to bring flowers from the town or from the highway on your way to Samadhi.

In those days all the windows, including the rear window, remained open without any fuss. The black and white framed photograph of Baba, which presently is in Baba's Cabin, was in front of us inside the Samadhi. The murals in those days were crumbling. At night the light behind the Samadhi would be switched on.

For years the outside walls of the Samadhi were painted white and so were the five emblems of the religions. (Baba was once asked about the Buddhist religion's symbol and He pointed to the top of the dome and said that this was the emblem for the Buddhist religion.) The four religious symbols had come from Bombay. I understand that Navroji Dadachanji, Chanji's brother and Arnavaz's and Rhoda's father, was a civil contractor, and following Baba's instructions, he completed constructed of the dome after many years of labour.

Finally a painting of Baba was approved by the women mandali and was installed in the Samadhi. Thus the rear window was closed forever. An American lady artist touched up the murals, which is a story in itself.

After Mansari's health failed, Rhoda and Jim Mistry took over the Samadhi artis. As the number of pilgrims grew, we started performing the artis with some Baba lovers inside the Samadhi as well as outside, and finally only outside. After Rhoda, Dolly Dastoor became the custodian of the artis. Sitting on the platforms on each side of the crypt was stopped.

The body of Baba's beloved Mehera was placed beside His, on His right. The gravestones for the women mandali started appearing, a couple at a time. Five on one side and four on the other. All were cremated except for Mehera.

Three good things have happened in the recent past. A device has been made which permits a wheelchair to go inside and chairs are allowed inside for seniors to sit on. During Amartithi, a barricade is put up at the entrance to the Samadhi to prevent pilgrims from taking too much time there, allowing more pilgrims to take darshan inside the Samadhi on January 31st itself. In the summer of 2006 a new route was opened between the Meher Pilgrim Retreat and the Samadhi.

The first mural on the right inside the Samadhi always reminds me of our mom, Khorshed Khan, being held by Beloved Baba at His bosom the first time we met Him. If anyone comes to the Samadhi crying, "I lost my child," I take them in and show them the dome where Baba is shown with a child. I tell them, "Your child is safe with Him."

The CCTV came into the Samadhi for security reason. Technology has come to our aid and now we can have LIVE darshan of the Samadhi in the comfort of our homes.

AVATAR MEHER BABA KI JAI

A Half Century of Samadhi

by Chris Barker

I first visited Baba's Samadhi in April 1969, when our darshan group, the Myrtle Beach flight, was loaded onto buses and taken on a bumpy ride in the summer heat from Poona to Meherabad.

Actually, I don't remember the heat. I was from Texas, so it seemed normal to me. Plus, I was so thrilled and happy to be there in Baba's home country and among the mandali—whom I had instantly come to love—that I didn't really notice the minor discomforts.

I think we walked up the hill to the Samadhi. Now, fifty years later, my memories of the details are vague. When I went into the Samadhi, I was awed to be in the place where the Avatar's body rested. I remember the ethereal murals. I bowed down, but I don't know if the engraved marble slab was there yet. Baba had only been put to rest in the Samadhi two and a half months earlier.

On that day we also saw Lower Meherabad, met Mohammad the mast and went to the Trust compound and Meherazad.

My experience of the 1969 darshan was that I was floating in Baba's love for much of the whole week. I was high as a kite from it and was so new to Baba that I thought that this was the way it was always going to be. Sweet!

A month after the darshan, I was drafted into the Army. By the end of 1969, I was in Viet Nam. I wasn't floating any more, but Baba's love carried me through that experience.

After the Army I went to college, changed majors two or three times and wound up getting a degree in geology. I went to work for a small, independent oil company in Houston and after a few years, eventually had enough money to go back to India.

In 1981, twelve long years after my original visit to the Samadhi, I was again back at Meherabad. As I walked up the hill to the Samadhi, I was filled with memories of that one-day visit in 1969. Now, however, I felt 'dried up.' But I was thrilled and happy to be back after so long!

During that stay, Baba gradually opened me up and filled me with His love again.

That visit was during Amartithi of 1981, and one experience in the Samadhi was particularly touching for me. I volunteered to help at Amartithi and was given a small cardboard badge to pin on my shirt. One evening I was asked to stand at the door of the Samadhi and admit people one-by-one in an orderly fashion. I had to keep looking in the Samadhi so that I would know when to admit the next person. Thus, I was seeing the expression on the face of each person just after they had Baba's darshan. Soon, this was like being at the door of a blast furnace—with the blast being Baba's love.

People had been standing in line for hours for their moment in the Tomb with Beloved Baba; many were very emotional. Watching them, my heart was opened and I suddenly felt a very strong wave of Baba's love wash over me. It was quite tangible, like a bolt of electricity, and it stunned and uplifted me. And then I remembered! This is what I had felt for much of the week at the 1969 darshan! It made me realize again how blessed I had been to be at that monumental event. Moreover, it vividly reminded me of the power and majesty of Baba's divine love and the reality of His godhood.

That visit to India in 1981 was particularly transformative. Baba filled me to the top with His love and I was a different person when I came back.

Over the years, there were more wonderful visits to India. Each, however, with fewer and fewer of Baba's precious mandali to welcome me home. Today, as I write this, I feel blessed beyond measure to have had the opportunity to sit at their feet and hear stories of the God-Man. From them I gained a hint of the fragrance of His advent—and countless practical tips on how to love Baba.

Half a century after my first visit, my wife Anne and I went back to India in November 2019. It had been seven long years since our last visit. I was prompted internally to go because there was a special program at Meherabad to commemorate the 50th anniversary of the 1969 darshan.

This time we traveled to a 'post-mandali' India. I participated in the anniversary program and then found that the focus of this trip was on taking darshan at Baba's Samadhi. Unlike the old days, there was not the pull of the mandali drawing me happily to Meherazad. Instead, I found my thrill on Meherabad Hill!

Every time I went to the Samadhi I felt Baba's love warming my heart. I felt deeply grateful for the opportunity of resting my hand on the black basalt blocks of the Samadhi walls as I stood in line near the door. I was so happy to go inside and lay my head at His feet. Each darshan, morning and evening, was like a dip in the pool of Baba's renewing love.

It was a simple life: darshan at the Samadhi; eat; think about Baba. Repeat.

Baba even gave us two extra weeks in India. Although, unfortunately, it was because Anne was in the hospital with pneumonia! Nonetheless, we did have more opportunities for darshan at the Samadhi and I was also able to attend the touching dhuni ceremony.

Little did we know, when we left India in mid-December 2019, that within two and a half months, the Samadhi would be closed and locked due to the worldwide Coronavirus pandemic of 2020. Now I feel profoundly grateful that Baba gave us this last (but hopefully not final) visit to His Samadhi!

Jai Baba!

A Lesson Only He Could Teach

by Winnie Barrett

Over the years with Meher Baba I made eight or nine trips to His home in India. During each journey I was bathed in the Divine Love of the Avatar of the Age. In the earlier days (the 1970s and '80s), whenever I went to Baba's Samadhi, there would only be twenty or twenty-five of us there, mostly Westerners. Nowadays there are long lines, fewer Westerners, many more Indians, and increasingly more people from all parts of the world. These days, we slowly inch our way up to the threshold, with a single rose in hand, or a garland of tuberose, or roses and marigolds, beautiful and sweet smelling, each adding subtle nuances to one another. The end result is a blissful lightheadedness, at times nearly overpowering.

Over these years, while at the Samadhi I observed women whose feelings overflowed as they approached the threshold of their Beloved. Some wiped tears from their eyes with their scarves, some put their hands on the Tomb's outside walls, or placed foreheads against the stones as if to merge with the Tomb itself. Others sat beneath the lean-to outside and quietly wept, their hearts brimming over with love, or conflict, sorrow or longing, whatever triggered their tears. I never let them know, and as I put these feelings onto paper now, I'm quite embarrassed at myself, but privately I thought of these expressions as "overly dramatic" and showy. Inwardly, I criticized them and secretly felt superior for not being so gushy. During my pilgrimage in 1997, I was feeling especially critical of several women, thinking their feelings weren't sincere, and that they were filled with ego. Well, that should have been a clue to me that Baba was up to something, but I wasn't paying attention.

Bal Natu had just had his book, *The Samadhi, Star of Infinity,* published and on a quiet afternoon, he came over from Meherazad to dedicate the book to Baba at the Samadhi itself. A small group of us went up the hill with him. We were mostly silent, or talking in hushed tones as we climbed the hill. When we arrived we slipped off our shoes and approached the threshold.

There, we said the prayers together. Some also recited them in other languages. As our voices blended in praise, in repentance and in asking Baba to help us love Him more and more, the atmosphere became charged—Beloved Baba's Presence emerged from within, first surrounding us, then steeping us in His love. I was overcome with emotion. Bursting into tears, I felt the urge to immerse myself in His Presence in whatever way I could. I stepped to the wall, first resting, then pressing my head into the rocks, weeping uncontrollably. My head, then my hands also pressed into the stone, trying to draw His Presence into every cell of my body, into every part of my being.

I don't know how long I stayed. By the time I returned to my surroundings, people were leaving. I slipped back into my shoes and descended the hill alone, humbled, amazed at myself. It wasn't until years later that I understood what a gift Baba had given me—new compassion

and acceptance of each individual's journey, new understanding of His ways, and help to trim my ego to a size
more pleasing to Him.

So I Said, "Yes, Baba."

by Brad Gunn

This is a more or less full accounting of what happened to me on the last three days of the Great Darshan in April 1969. Only a small amount of it applies to my moments in the Samadhi, but the events leading up to my Samadhi experience are relevant so I include them here.

On the morning that we were to visit Meherabad and Meherazad, we all arose early and mustered at the Poona Club. There we encountered numerous buses that would take us to the Samadhi. At that time, 5 A.M., I felt okay. But at about 8:30 A.M., we stopped at a "resting place," a large public bus stand, and I got down to use the WC. By then I was not feeling great, having a bit of fever, and also loose stools. Using my first public WC in India was an experience, the hardest part of which was in keeping my pants from touching the floor. Anyway, traveling with us on the bus was a young Indian doctor who was charged with looking after our health. I mentioned to him when I got back to the bus that I was feeling a bit poorly and had a bit of fever. He immediately gave me two or three pills and said, "Take these." Which I did.

Now, at this time I was a twenty-two year-old hippy who had come to Baba two years earlier and had not done any drugs since becoming a Baba-lover, as per His order. None, and I was somewhat proud of that. So looking back on it I find it astounding that at the moment the doctor gave me the pills, I simply took them and didn't ask what they were. Only afterwards did I enquire, and he told me, "Some analgesic and also some barbiturate." "(Expletive) wonderful!" I thought—"I'm going to show up at Baba's Tomb stoned on Seconal or whatever barb the doctor had given me. Baba's joke of course, but I was really pissed off at myself for not having asked first.

About an hour later we pulled up at lower Meherabad and got off the bus. By this point I was running a raging fever and felt really terrible, but we all walked up the hill to the Tomb. The temperature was probably 110 F and the sun was typically full-on Indian sun. So we formed a long queue to enter Baba's Samadh, but with no shade of any kind available. (In those days there were no structures around the Tomb and no trees.) I couldn't take standing in the direct sun any longer, so I walked over to Mansari's kitchen and lay down on the floor by her hearth.

It was probably over an hour later that Marshall Haye came to find me and told me that the queue for the Tomb had cleared now, and I should go take darshan because everyone was ready to head back down the hill to the buses. So I got up and managed to walk to the Samadhi.

When I entered the Tomb it was amazing. Overwhelming was really more to the point, the vibration being so powerful. But when I bowed down at Baba's feet, I was immediately overcome with such force, such power! And I instantly got the message from Him that I was going to pass out if I lingered there, and were I to pass out, all the Baba lovers waiting outside the Samadhi were going to attach great spiritual significance to that, which it didn't deserve. So I said "Yes, Baba," and managed to get back up and leave the Samadhi.

The rest of the story doesn't really matter that much, though there are a couple of amusing anecdotes to it. Perhaps I looked as sick as I felt at that moment, because someone took charge of me and got me down the hill. We first went to the Trust Compound, where they put me on a bed in the corridor just outside of Adi's office, and put a glass of water on a stool beside the bed. But before I could drink the water one of the compound dogs came in and beat me to it. Then I fell in and out of sleep for a while, only to be briefly awoken by Adi yelling at some pilgrim to stop bowing down at the bed I was in because Baba never slept on it!

So I never got to Meherazad that trip. Eventually they packed me and a pregnant woman suffering from heat stroke into a taxi to carry us back to Poona, and they made arrangements for me to switch places with my brother John and stay with Barbara, John's wife at the Poona Club. And then that evening Dr. Donkin arrived to check on my condition. He gave me medication, told me to drink lots of water and with luck I probably wouldn't die, though were I an Indian, whatever it was I had, generally killed about fifty percent of the people who got it. He had a name for it, and it was some specific kind of dysentery, but I can't remember what it was.

Jai Meher Baba

Mansari's Samadhi Story

by Greg Harland

During my first visit to India in late 1969 I stayed for over three months with the mandali. Much of that time I was living in Meherabad with Padri and Mansari. I usually spent mornings with Padri and the afternoons with Mansari. The time with Mansari was often spent hearing many of her personal stories about life with Baba. One story she told me was quite unusual and I'll do my best to repeat it as accurately as I can.

Mansari said that every morning she would go to the Tomb, unlock the door, clean the Tomb, and decorate it with fresh flowers.

Before I go on, I'd like to share an experience I had related to that daily task. One morning I got there early enough to witness this ritual. I got to the Tomb just before Mansari came out and the night watchman was still there sleeping at the door of the Tomb. His head was resting on the threshold with a hatchet for a pillow. He was very dark skinned and when he opened his eyes they were very bright and blue. When he stared at me I can honestly say I was intimidated. When Mansari came out they seemed to communicate with looks and not words. As she approached he stood up, picked up the hatchet, continuing to stare at me and stepped back while Mansari stepped up and unlocked the door. Mansari looked in and indicated everything was okay. Then the watchman quietly walked away, while still keeping a close eye on me.

Back to the story. Mansari said one morning she woke up and felt an urgent need to go quickly to the Tomb. As she got there she realized she had forgotten to bring the keys, so she went to the door, which had a three-link lock chain that allowed her to push it open about two inches. She pushed the door open and through the crack she said she saw Baba's white sadra brush by the door. She called through the door, *Baba, Baba is that You?* No answer, so she ran back to her kitchen and got the keys to open the Tomb. When she opened the door she saw the dirt was collapsed into a hole. She also said the Tomb inside had an intense smell of roses. She said over the next week the scent of roses spread over the entire hill. During that time thousands of Indians who had heard about this came to visit Baba's Tomb.

Baba Drops His Body

by Jimmy Khan

On 31st January 1969 at around 7 P.M. my mother, Khorshed Khan, returned from work. Normally she would return at around 8 P.M. and I wondered why so early today. She walked in and said, "Meher Baba is no more." We were stunned. I was writing my paper and my hand froze. No one, not even the mandali ever thought that one day Baba would be gone. We thought that He would be there for us forever as He was the God-Man, not just a man. "Did you hear what I said? Get up and pack up your bag, we are going to Nagar now," Mom said. We were told that Baba's body would be interred at around 8 in the morning.

A group of His lovers from Mumbai led by Jal and Dolly Dastoor took the night train from Mumbai. Some were wailing and inconsolable. One was trying to pacify the other. At around 8 in the morning we were still far from Ahmednagar. Knowing that Baba's body would be covered at any time now, we performed the arti in the train. Jal had requested the train driver and the guard to stop the train at lower Meherabad, so we could alight right there, in order to be able to reach Baba's Samadhi in time, in case there was any delay in the covering of His body.

Finally the train stopped at Meherabad and we got down, helping the old ladies with the bags and night beddings. We carried only one change of clothes as we were to return the next day, since Baba's body was to be enclosed the next morning. We went up the hill—this was my first visit ever to Meherabad. We met Eruch uncle. "Do not meet with any one—first go inside the Samadhi and have Baba's darshan," Eruch uncle told the group.

There must have been a sigh of relief on the faces of all who heard this, which effectively meant that the Beloved's body was still not interred. I still couldn't believe it. One by one we entered the Samadhi, went down the four steps, touched Baba's feet and came up again. His body was wrapped in a white cloth and rested on a wooden plank on plain earth. Then we met the men mandali. The women went and met the female mandali, who were in the water tower, and they stayed there too.

I and the other men stayed down the hill at lower Meherabad in the mandali hall. As His lovers started pouring in, the first ones occupied the limited space in the hall and those who came later slept on the front and rear verandah. Space started getting hard to find. As I returned in the afternoon for a little rest, my bag and bedding had been tossed elsewhere and I had to scout around for them. The exercise of searching would be repeated at night. Padri kaka supplied the morning tea. Our food came from Ahmednagar—the Trust fed us all.

Up on the Hill Baba's body lay in the crypt. Though it was the first week of February the afternoons got hot and stuffy. The Samadhi, being made of stone, got especially hot. Lovers fanned Baba's body, trying to keep it cool. Slabs of ice surrounded Him. Sawdust and black salt kept the ice going. I helped Jal Dastoor with this chore. The doctors inspected His body twice a day to ensure that there were no signs of decay. If there were, they would ask for the enclosing of the body immediately.

At one point, Sarosh Irani made an announcement requesting lovers to leave Meherabad if they had had darshan—funds were running dry as the Trust had to feed them all. At this point the Parsi group from Bombay got together and passed the hat around among themselves and gave the purse to Sarosh. Maybe this was the first ever donation received by the Trust.

Mom and I were at Meherabad but my sisters, Diana, her husband, Manchi and Bapsy had stayed in Bombay. Diana was in the second week of her new job at Tata Consultancy Services (TCS), which was not easy to get. When Mom sent word from Meherabad that Baba's body was still open for viewing, and that they should not miss this opportunity of a lifetime, Diana could not hold back any longer. She went to her boss and told her, just as offering information, that Baba had dropped His body and that it was still open for viewing, and her mom and brother were at Ahmednagar. Her boss was very spiritually inclined and asked Diana to go to pay her last respects and she told her to go right away. That same night the three of them took the train for Ahmednagar. The next morning they were in the crypt.

We were among those who fanned Baba's beloved body. We also sat in turns on the side tiles in the crypt. On one such occasion Bapsy saw Baba open His eyes. This was no hallucination. She was petrified, dropped the fan and almost ran out. This was so unusual that she kept this to herself for years for fear of being ridiculed. Years later we would sit with Mansari for hours in her room, and on one such sitting, Mansari told the Khans that one Parsi priest entered the Samadhi when Baba's body was in the crypt. As there were others in front of him, he craned his neck and tried to see Baba's body. To his utter amazement he saw Baba raise Himself to enable the priest to see Him. This was narrated by the priest himself to Mansari. On hearing this Bapsy gathered courage to narrate her story and Mansari endorsed her story saying that the priest and Bapsy were not alone. I too, once saw Baba's eyes flickering as I fanned His body. Mom also had this experience.

The scene at the hill was somber and sad. Occasionally someone would go into hysterics, frenzy and wailing, and those around would console each other. Twice a day the women mandali would come out and walk up to the Samadhi. They were heartbroken and shattered. They refused to accept that Baba was no more in the body. They deluded themselves that He was in a coma and would rise again.

Adi Irani, Baba's secretary at the Trust office in the town, was swamped with telephone calls and cables from lovers, wanting to know whether Baba's body was still open for darshan and could they still come? Adi Irani gave them a stock answer, "Come if you wish, Baba's body is still uncovered, but it could be enclosed any moment. It all depends on the doctors. Take your pick if you so wish. But there's no guarantee." Some came, some did not.

It was finally decided to enclose Baba's body on the 7th of February 1969, which happened to be His birthday according to the Zoroastrian calendar. I went up the hill in the morning and had darshan once more for the nth and last time. Lovers were asked to take their last darshan as the time got closer, and finally the announcement came that the darshan was now closed and the body would be covered and enclosed. Mass hysteria took over and lovers could not accept that the game was over for all time. Mayhem let loose. Every one wanted to have a last look, and there was an ensuing rush towards the Samadhi. I distinctly remember there were three cops who started wielding their lathis (batons) to disperse the crowd, though not so aggressively so as to injure anyone. Emotions were at a crest.

I realized the futility of being in the midst of it all. Baba had given me more than ample chances to be so close to Him these last seven days on the hill. I thought it best to sit away from it all in peace and quietude. I moved away towards the water tower and sat in the hollow doorway, now the entrance to the museum. Hardly a minute had passed, when Meheru aunty from the women mandali saw me seated there. She asked me to take from her hands a basket full of red roses, which were to be laid on the Beloved's body before His body was enclosed—roses from Mehera. With the basket in my hand, I went behind the Baba cabin and behind the Samadhi. shouting, "Side please, please move, make way please, flowers from Mehera for Baba, please make way." The lovers turned their heads and instinctively stepped aside. It was like Moses parting the Red Sea as I made my way right up to the Samadhi. Not a rose fell from the basket and neither was I jostled.

I saw Jal Dastoor inside the Samadhi door and said, "Jal, these roses are from Mehera to be laid on Baba before He is covered." Having taken the flowers, Jal said, "Jimmy, get the earth." For the past seven days I had not seen any earth near the Samadhi so I said, "What earth?" "Don't you see the earth on your left?" Jal roared. On 31st January Padri kaka was given the task of making the arrangement at the Samadhi. He organized the digging up of the crypt floor, which had been covered and tiled. The excavated earth was stored, then brought on the morning of the 8th and kept where today Mehera's Tomb is, to cover Baba's body again—all of which I was not aware. I grabbed a spade and a ghamela (a shallow metal pan), filled it with the first clumps of earth and gave it to Jal. "Get more!" Jal shouted. At this time others took over for me. Having done my job, I went back to the quiet doorway. This pair of hands have been blessed to take the last roses to cover His body from Mehera, and to spread the first pan of earth over the wooden box covering His body too. I must have done something good.

I still wonder to this day how many of His lovers know how His body was enclosed. I believe and I hope *Lord Meher* covers this aspect. Baba's body was wrapped in white cloth and placed on a wooden plank, the lid of a hard board box, made, say 6' by 2' by 2' and open on one side. The box was flipped over to cover His body. The crypt was then filled with the earth, as you fill a pit with a coffin in it. Darshan must have been opened again for His lovers to have one last darshan before they left Meherabad. The next day the Bombay group met with the mandali. Eruch uncle said, "You are also going?" The group said, "We had come for a day and stayed for eight days. Now you all are also going to Meherazad." The Bombay group was the last to have left Meherabad, except for the mandali and maybe a few Ahmednagar locals.

It was generally perceived even by the mandali that Baba went out like a light. He gave no sign, no indication whatsoever, of His imminent passing on. Well, not true and not fair. Baba did drop hints, but nobody understood.

If the mandali and His lovers could not understand the hints dropped by Baba, it is only because our perception of time and our language and His language were different. Nobody, including the mandali, wanted to take the hints.

8th February 1969 ended the Khan family tryst with the physical connection with the Avatar of the Age. A chapter in our lives ended.

A Twist to the Tale

by Darab Satha as written by Jimmy Khan

In the not so distant past I came across Darab Sathha from the Sathha family. Darab has passed on since. This is Darab's story.

Darab came from Ahmednagar where he and his family were very close to Baba and the mandali. Darab was very special to Baba and he and Baba would spend long hours closeted in a room together, just the two of them. He was *that* special. As Ahmednagar offered no college, education or employment, he migrated to Bombay.

On 1st February 1969, Darab was having his bath early in the morning. His cousin who stayed with him knocked at the bathroom door and shouted, "Darab, Meher Baba dropped His body yesterday and He is to be interred this morning." Darab could not believe what he heard. He started weeping and wailing. "Baba, how could you do this?" He was then told that the whole Bombay group had left the previous night for Ahmednagar. This added salt to the fresh wounds.

Darab started crying uncontrollably. His chance to see his Beloved for the last time ever was also lost. Nobody from the Bombay Centre or Ahmednagar had bothered to inform him. Darab then saw a vision of Meher Baba enter from the bathroom window. Darab moaned, "Baba how could You go? How could You have just gone away leaving us?" Baba said, "Why are you crying? Do not cry—go to Meherabad and tell the mandali not to enclose my body till the 7th." Darab said, "Baba, but You are already to be covered by 9 A.M. and who will believe me? Who am I? How will they trust me? They will ridicule me." Baba said, "My body will still be uncovered when you arrive. Go and give them my message."

Darab left for Ahmednagar. On reaching the hill he found that Baba's body was still uncovered. Darab approached Eruch uncle and confided in him about the vision and message he'd had. Had it been any other person, Eruch uncle would have chided him and maybe dismissed him as hallucinating. But Eruch uncle knew Darab's spiritual status. He asked him to wait and called Mani and one more mandali member and asked Darab to repeat what he had said. They trusted Darab's every word and called the doctors.

Dr. Ginde, the top of the line neurosurgeon from Bombay attending to Baba, lost his cool. "Who is this guy talking such rubbish? He must be hallucinating." Eruch uncle and the others had to pacify him. Darab intervened to say that once a saintly person who had a following, had passed on, and his body was left uncovered by his followers for a month and no deterioration had happened to his body—and Meher Baba was not just a saintly person.

Darab stated, "It is my duty to tell you this message from Baba." Dr. Ginde washed his hands of it. He said that he was a doctor and his reputation was on the line. He could not be a silent spectator—at the very first sign of any decomposition, he would quit. This was an ultimatum. The mandali decided to keep the body uncovered till the 7th, of February, provided the body was free of decomposition. It held.

Writing in the Tomb

by Stephen Paul Miller

"In this book," Francis Brabazon prefaces *Stay with God*, "I have tried to offer some praise to one who has not so much 'changed the course of my life' as given it sanction." Before meeting Baba, Francis said, "His (own) religion was a quest for beauty, what it is, and its relation to truth." One of the manifestations of his passion was writing. Francis said that Baba "proved" the Truth and Beauty motivating him. This gave the poet the ultimate authorization to keep doing what he had been doing on a whole other level.

My story isn't quite like that. But looking back upon my experiences on Samadhi Hill, it feels as if Baba was doing something for me, though of course, I can't know. In the early seventies, I'd sit in the Tomb writing poetry that went all over the place. These poems make sense to me now, but at that time I wasn't then going for "sense." This is the kind of poetry I was writing in the Tomb:

ALREADY SHUFFLED

It was so peaceful
as if to correspond with a chance I had lost
but is all this revolving around myself
trying to get away from something
and if gray is the pure tone
am I the greener tensions
anxiously compressed?

Flying around with these little bugs
Why must my discoveries always be negative
    (to discover what you hadn't been doing,
      who cares what you've done)
or bypassing the customs official I'm harassed
or just in general feeling like a sandy
vegetable, in retrospect a trodden salad?

The peace has already turned into a cave-in
as if God's impatience were my guilt
but most of all I feel I've missed a chance,
many chances in fact form a pattern
which coming in retrospect seems a shadow.

I think people were complaining about me writing in the
Tomb, and I suspect that had something to do with the
prohibition against writing inside the Tomb soon thereafter.

As the above poem indicates, I was nervous about my future. Few make a living as a poet, but I wasn't particularly suited for anything else, if even that. I had all kinds of ideas that weren't for me, such as going to architecture school. In the Tomb, I silently asked Baba what I should do. I would do whatever I felt Baba wanted. Then I heard Baba more clearly then ever before. It was a real voice, a little like mine, but silent and speaking inside me. The *exact* words were, "You can do whatever you want to do, but I want you to be a writer." This was strange. It was unlike anything I'd think on my own or would even have considered. Writing and poetry were completely different to me. I couldn't even write term papers. I was a poet, not a writer. I had no interest in "writing" itself. I immediately noted the oddity of the word "writing."

I kept hearing what I heard Baba say He wanted. It seemed to me that He was saying He wanted me to continue in my own peculiar fashion what He'd already chosen for me, but change just enough to meet the world halfway. I may write poetry on my own terms, but I would also have to write on the world's terms. I had to have confidence in my ability to write whatever the world put before me, because whatever the world put in front of me was one manifestation of Baba and what I had to (un)learn.

In retrospect, it was integral to my development that I feel more comfortable writing discursively. I needed a cohesive medium to "unwind" in. I might still have the same problems I have always had, but I was perhaps just slightly less attached to them. For instance, when angry I could more often avoid acting on that anger by putting my emotions and thoughts into words and to that extent having power over them.

Still, I was nervous. Being a writer seemed only slightly more practical than being a poet. I asked Eruch if I should get a Ph.D. and he said, "Yes. Baba doesn't want you to be a bum." I found Eruch to be more or less right about everything. Yet being an out of work Ph.D. wasn't much more practical than being a poet.

After a while, I went up to the Tomb and asked Baba exactly what He wanted me to do. I had my eyes closed but opened them because I thought I heard something. In a firm but reassuring "outside voice" that was inside me, I heard, "You can do whatever you want to do, but I want you to get a Ph.D. in American Civilization at N.Y.U." (New York University). I thought it was strange for Baba to say "American civilization" because when Gandhi was in London he was asked what he thought about Western Civilization, and he famously replied, "I think it would be a good idea."

Why did Baba want me to get a Ph.D. in American Civilization? I think because it allowed me to express myself and that allowed me to succeed at it. Going into an interdisciplinary field allowed me to make uncanny comparisons and see the same forces at work in entirely different fields. I could be scholarly and based in the world, but at the same time poetic and yet relevant.

I wrote a dissertation seeing the '70s through Watergate, John Ashbery's "Self-Portrait in a Convex Mirror," seventies film and Jasper Johns' mid-seventies crosshatch paintings. I found a polarization we're still experiencing. It was fun. The dissertation was published by a major university press, and it led me to become a tenured full professor, free to teach "creative writing," poetry, film, and culture. It's not perfect, but it's fun. And when life has posed what seemed like momentous problems, I could devote myself to them without worrying about job security. I think Baba knew what He was doing.

millers@stjohns.edu

What's the Use?

by Susan Herr

In the early '70s we could sit or even lie down in Baba's Tomb. So I used to spend many hours doing that. One day Eruch happened to be up there. Since he encouraged us to spend as much time in the Tomb as possible, I stopped him and asked, "What's the use of sitting in the Tomb all day if all I think about is what we are we having for dinner or what will I wear to dinner, etc."

He answered, "You don't have to be aware of the sun for it to warm you, so get back in there!"

Divine Desperation or
In the Blink of an Eye

by Jack Burke

It was November 1972 when I arrived for the first time in Meherabad. This, after an overwhelming, completely draining and life changing three years of searching day and night from California to New York and back again for an "answer" to what life on this planet was all about! After the experience on March 31st of the same year, the face to FACE meeting with Meher Baba, here I was one morning leaving Viloo's Villa and planning on spending three nights in Meherabad, with two or three male companions.

I remember walking slowly up the hill, thinking, "My God, God walked this path so many times, that here I am tromping over His footprints, again and again. Only His infinite compassion can allow that, never mind the sacred sanctity of the Samadhi."

Both inside the Samadhi, as well as in the atrium, there were day visitors as well, going in, bowing down to His feet, sitting on the floor or up on the sides or leaving. My only recollection is putting my shoeless right foot on the threshold and stepping up with my other foot. An act, that is prohibited today, mainly in an attempt to preserve under polyurethane coating, that piece of carved teakwood from being worn down by the millions of feet that will eventually step into this Holy of Holies.

Time stopped. I stopped, caught as if in a time warp! From the bottom of my feet to the top of my head I erupted without restraint. The sobs and tears of both agony and ecstasy went on and on. I felt my whole being turned inside and out. All the energy and years of searching, perhaps even the countless millenniums of walking, wandering, worrying and wondering about God, expunged from my being and landed at His Feet, like some Divine Regurgitation.

The upshot of the whole experience came when I approached a few of the other pilgrims and began apologizing for disrupting their communion with the Master. There was a pregnant pause as they looked at me askance. One woman looked me right in the eye and said: "What are you talking about?" I began to reply, then stopped. I mean, can you see a grown man explaining to someone: "You mean to tell me that neither of you saw or heard me sobbing and crying as I stood on the threshold blocking the doorway?" No, I think not! As far as I'm concerned the Master stopped time for them and expanded the moment for me all in the blink of an eye.

In February, 1987, Marvin Johnson and I were each given a round trip ticket to Meherabad by Tommy Brustman's Dad, Wendell. This was in thanks for the three years' work on Dr. Deshmukh's 8mm film of Meher Baba's work with some of the hundreds of masts. So, after a fourteen year absence, I returned to walk once again in the footprints of my Master.

Staying at the Meher Pilgrim Center, I came in contact with a pilgrim who was returning from doing night watchman duty on the Hill. After a brief conversation it became obvious that this was something I could also do if the timing was right. And it was! By going up the Hill and contacting Mansari, I was granted five straight nights of watchman duty. Again, one reaches the limits of words, because at that time still, the degree of silence and nighttime lighting in the surrounding areas had not even approached the level it is today. What was it like? I offer the following ghazal, rendered the morning after.

O Saki, What Kind of Bartender Are You!

O Beloved,

Such a marvelous boon to me You have granted
To watch over Your Tavern through these nights so enchanted
While nothing I hear can dispel Your Silence so thunderous
Pervading my every moment under starlight so wondrous.

In this, the center of Your universe I humbly stand
Feel Your love pouring out to my outstretched hand
Yet with eyes downcast, feet planted firm, I wonder
anew
When my turn will come to be a bartender like You.

The Word has gone out across oceans so vast
As You wait to serve those whom You've caught
    In the love-net You cast
In the dawning day they come and implore
All these drunks crawling to Your Tavern door.

But, what is this You have turned me into?
What have I become?
They take me for a watchman
But I know I'm just another drunken bum.

So, round Your Tavern store I walk
And I know You just laugh
At this drunken fool who shuffles and stumbles
With thumping wooden staff.

O Saki, what kind of bartender are You, anyway?
How can I be the bouncer when You ply me with wine
I've become so intoxicated
It's only for another glass that I pine.

Where am I, what in God's name did You do?
It seemed the whole night was filled
With the aroma of Your delicious brew.

Ah! Yes, This must be the place, this spiritual bowery
To become drunk on Your love
The price of the wedding dowry.

My heart reels, I sit dazed on Your sidewalk
I can't think, nor see straight, nor can I talk
I lurch, I stumble, I rattle Your Tavern door

My body trembles, my heart cries out
One more! One more!

O Saki, don't deny me, don't turn off the tap
Let me have just a wee one
Just pour it in my lap
For I'll wait here forever until it's all said and done!

O lover of My wine

For the likes of you
Saki's Tavern is ever open
And the drinks are on the house
For Love must respond to love
And Saki never turns away
A love-drunk souse.

Only This Moment

by Nancy Friedemann

In 1972 I was staying in Ahmednagar with Sarosh and Viloo for a month. At that time I was the only pilgrim in their home, Viloo Villa. They were wonderfully kind and fun to be with, treating me as they did their daughter, Freny, who happened to be there also.

Sarosh would invite me to go with him where he needed to go, and it was always a surprise event. So it wasn't unusual, after dinner on the last evening of my trip, when Sarosh said, "Come on, let's go."

It was just at dusk when we arrived at the foot of the hill to Baba's Samadhi. I had two secret wishes—to hear the Arangaon qawaali singers, and to be alone in the Samadhi with Baba. As we walked slowly up the hill, I realized that the qawaali singers were there at the Samadhi, and that Sarosh and I were the only visitors. As the evening became darker, the singers quietly packed up and left.

I was alone in a deep Indian night in Meher Baba's Samadhi. Time passed as I sat in stillness, in profound silence.

The silence was suddenly broken by a thundering rain crashing down on the hill. I came out of the Samadhi where Sarosh was waiting. We headed down the hill in drenching rain and in squelching red-orange mud. There seemed to be a light shining through every raindrop. The air was cool and refreshing.

I wanted to stay there forever with the rain pouring down, twirling and singing, running barefoot in the mud. It was the eternal, infinite *now*—the hill, the drenching rain, the mud, the moment—*only this moment.*

At Last!

by Jacko Caraco

It was the beginning of March 1973, my first trip to India. Arriving at the Samadhi, I was met by Nana Kher and the "Welcome Home Embrace." I entered the Samadhi and bowed down. When my head touched the marble the thought-image-couplet came to me—

I dove through a needle's eye into a pool of infinity...there is a treasure here I want to share with the whole world; but I don't know how!?

To me, that tiny Tomb in the middle of nowhere was like a dot in the center of the whole vast universe and a door to the infinite, and I had found it at last!!!

Baba Makes Me Forget Who I Am

by Priti Zamre

I was born into a Baba family, so of course Baba came into my life from my birth. Baba says, "It behooves My lovers not to attribute miracles to Me." Yet it seems there are innumerable miracles performed by Him in my day to day life.

The most remarkable thing that happens to me every time I visit the Tomb is that Beloved Baba makes me forget who I am in this material world. And believe me, this has happened to me since my childhood. I was in absolute forgetfulness of which grade I was studying in, what my school's name was, in fact, who my family was, even my mom and dad. I was never afraid about being left alone at Baba's Samadhi.

When I wasn't married, even then I would come to Baba's Samadhi to pour all my memories good and bad, all my happenings to my Divine Mother. If I intended it or not, tears would start flowing continuously, whether there was nothing on my mind, or if I was remembering all my actions, words and thoughts that might have displeased our Beloved.

And now, I come to His Samadhi with my child and the same feeling still continues—I forget everything related to me, I forget myself. While coming away from the Samadhi, I feel totally recharged afresh. Baba's connection with me goes back ages ago and I feel that no one and nothing really matters when I meet the Personification of Love.

Sometimes it's simply Baba being like a wine tender, filling my vessel, which is my heart, to the brim, and it overflows from my eyes in the form of tears, making me unaware of what is going on with me. And Baba is telling me, "I have so much Love to give; all you need to do is to empty your heart of all low desires of lust, greed, anger, and backbiting. I am all ready to fill up your heart with the abundance of Love, as I am the Ocean."

Jai Baba!

Amarthiti Tomb Duty

by Jon Meyer

In January 2013 I traveled to Meherabad, Maharashtra, India in anticipation of Amarthiti (the Celebration of the One Who Never Dies—the day that Beloved Avatar Meher Baba dropped His body to live in the hearts of His lovers). At first thousands, then tens of thousands of His lovers came from all over the globe to pay their respects at His Tomb-Shrine (Samadhi). I asked if I could serve on Samadhi duty, and was accepted to do so. There were a number of volunteer duties in and around Baba's Tomb. Among them were giving prasad [an Indian food or sweet consumed after worship], keeping the long line moving outside the Tomb, aiding His lovers to step in and out of His Tomb, helping with the numerous garlands devotees brought for Tomb placement, running messages, etc.

Meher Baba's Tomb was built under His instructions in 1938, more than thirty years before He dropped His body. It is a stone structure about ten feet by fifteen feet with a dome, and a polished stone floor. On the top corners of the outside walls are symbols of the world's religions. That dome, and the inside walls are beautifully painted in the Expressionist style by Helen Dahm, a prominent Swiss artist from the construction time. The paintings contain scenes of Meher Baba with villagers and devotees, depicting life in the local, rural area of India. In a number of places, the protrusions of the rough-cut stone walls were incorporated into the painted images. Inside lies a marble slab with Baba's quote inscribed, "I have not come to teach but to awaken." Beneath the marble slab lies Meher Baba's earthly remains. Pilgrims travel from all over the globe to visit this Tomb-shrine. Early every morning, devotees arrive to lovingly clean this Tomb with small cloths and sponges. They then lay down fresh flowers and garlands as a love offering to Him for the day. Frequently, garlands in the shape of a large heart are placed on the marble, and then filled with flower offerings from His lovers as they bow down inside to pay their respects to Him.

I remembered my first entrance into His Tomb in 1973. I waited in line. It didn't take long. There were devotees who clearly wanted some time with Him in His Tomb. When my turn came, I went in and sat down beside the marble slab. I wondered if Meher Baba would make His presence known. I closed my eyes and it seemed that I was in a long dark corridor.

Then far away at the end, a door cracked open, and out flooded the same intense white light that I had experienced on my first day on the Meher Center in Myrtle Beach, South Carolina, meeting Meher's brilliance through Darwin Shaw two years earlier. It was all consuming, and lifted me up until I could vaguely see the Samadhi and the pilgrims below. I was buoyed on a fount of the most beautiful light. I was whole. The Avatar of the Age was bathing me in blissful all-consuming love. I thought my life was complete—no need to prove or accomplish anything. If I died that moment, it would be fine, and my life was fulfilled.

Back in '73, this was just the inner door cracked open ever so slightly. The eternal beyond was behind that door. I wanted to fling the door open, but before I could, I had a thought. "What would the others think if I did that?" At that moment, the door closed, and I was back sitting on the floor of His Samadhi.

For my Amartithi Tomb duty in 2013, I was assigned to stand inside Baba's Tomb to help Baba lovers bow down and get up, and gently keeping the pilgrims moving in and out. My turn came for my assignment. I stood just inside Baba's Tomb on the right side and helped pilgrims from infants with their mothers to the very elderly step in and out. Some were able and quick. Others were infirm and needed assistance to bow or kneel. There were about eight to ten people in the Tomb at a time, with one at a time bowing down toward Him for a few seconds. But what an intense, powerful waterfall of love was flowing!

After experiencing the indescribable blast of love from hundreds of souls, my life's moments of conscious successes and failures were blurred by bliss. At first my mind would flash to past events in my life: *What hugs Mani gave, Eruch's stories in Mandali Hall at Meherazad, Laura Delivigne (a Sufi initiated by Inayat Kahn teaching me to bake bread in her home in Myrtle Beach), Kitty's stories of the ashram in India, Bhauji's advice, the amazing generosity of Baba lovers, focus on Him and wandering from focus on Him, the first thrush's song in Vermont spring, waking up at my desk and realizing the words I wrote after I dozed were better than ones written while awake, Deborah's devotion to The Beloved, the magic of the first time as a child when I mixed yellow paint with red and got orange...* Even my most inspired life instants first blended, then were consumed by all pervading Amarthiti Tomb bliss. But I forced myself to focus on my present duty.

Some had traveled thousands of miles by plane, train, bus, car, and some on foot. They were from many diverse backgrounds and nationalities, Hindus, Sikhs, Buddhists, Muslims, Christians, Parsis, Jews, Zoroastrians, rich and poor, educated and uneducated, some new to Him and some old lovers, a few I knew and many I didn't know, but felt love for anyway. My love for these strangers was prompted by their outpouring of fervent love for Lord Meher, and His for them. When one is bathed in bliss, there is no choice but to imbibe and pass it on.

> "One has to go beyond the mind to experience the spiritual bliss of desirelessness."
> —Meher Baba.

This is natural and comes without effort or thought. A few pilgrims were curious, but most were there to express their innermost love for Him. Some walked from far away in India, and some from close by came to bow down to Him in His Samadhi. The intense feelings of love from Him were palpable. Waves of love, bliss, and devotion were flowing from these lovers up, around, out of the Tomb, and into the sky. I was being saturated with love from all sides from many people at once. Outside, thousands of souls were focused on their turn to pour out their hearts to the Beloved.

When my duty time was supposed to be up, the next volunteer did not arrive, so I was asked to continue! More and more waves of fervent love and bliss permeated everything. I experienced the overwhelming love radiating from His lovers. I would look into each one's eyes and see tears of joy in many of them. More people—hundreds and hundreds streamed in, bowed down, and moved out again, each pouring out their love for Him, and He was showering the ecstasy from the Ancient One on them in return. He was clearly very much alive in the hearts of His lovers.

By the time my double Tomb duty was over, I was overwhelmed. I had managed to keep focus on my duty, but now I staggered out of His Samadhi, and tried to head back toward the Meher Pilgrim Retreat (MPR), where I was staying. This Samadhi time was more than 'following' Meher Baba, more than any emotion, more than any teaching or religion. This was His incredible gift of love for me and for so many others. It filled me up so completely that I could absorb nothing more. No gift could be greater.

I was love stunned. The world was gone! All that was left was the blast of love from a very long stream of aspirants/pilgrims. I had used up all my energy to focus on my duty for hours, and to not let the immense, vigorous spirit of love from so many wash my duty away. I now had a difficult time thinking or walking. I stood outside His Tomb, dazed when an old man came over and introduced himself. He said he was Shalig Ram Sharma from Hamirpur (then in his nineties, twenty-five years my senior).* He had met Meher Baba decades earlier. Now he said to me, "Brother, you look like you could use some help. I can see your time in Baba's Samadhi has soaked you in His love." He took my elbow and guided me slowly back across a field to where I was staying at the Meher Pilgrim Retreat.

***

* I found out later from reading Bal Natu's book *Tales of Meher Baba's Love* that Baba once asked Shalig Ram to tell Him whatever he had in his heart. He replied, "Baba, if You are to give, give me complete self-surrender, give me Your shelter, and give me the capacity." At that moment Baba raised His right hand with two fingers pointing upwards. Simultaneously there was a profuse flash of lightning and a loud peal of thunder filled the room. Baba gestured, *Khuda* [God] has heard your voice; everything is granted and this is its proof.

—From *Tales of Meher Baba's Love*, by Bal Natu, AMBPPCT, India © 2001 quoting from Glow International, November 1994.

Samadhi Story

by Barb and Ken Richstad

Witnessed and Narrated by Barb:

We biked out in the dark from Ahmednagar to Mehera-bad as usual for morning arti. In the early seventies we could stand in line on each side of the marble slab for the prayers and songs. I was standing on the left side, about two people behind Kenny, when right in the middle of the "American Arti" he fell forward, ramrod straight and unconscious, right onto the marble slab, crashing his forehead on the word "Beloved."

Hustle and bustle ensued, and Kenny, now barely conscious, was hauled out of the Samadhi.

Mansari cackled, "I guess Baba didn't like the way Ken was bowing down to Him and decided to give him a good yank."

Padri came rushing up the hill from Lower Meherabad. He pushed through the small crowd on the verandah, ignored Kenny lying on the floor, and threw himself across the marble slab, wiping Ken's blood off and rubbing the marble with his hands to make sure there were no cracks.

A car arrived, we bundled Ken in and drove him to the hospital in Ahmednagar. His canvas stretcher was set down for awhile onto the slate floor near a large antiquated x-ray machine. Next we met the doctor, a cheery fellow oblivious to the small bird building a nest in the upper corner of his office. "Lucky for you, you have a thick skull," he said. But he kept Ken at the hospital for the day, just in case.

Ken was placed in the "English Room"—down a narrow ward, crowded with Indian families and into a large room, where breezes flowed through barred windows and curtains were printed with tea-pots. A dog strolled through the hospital room and out again.

Ken is sometimes asked the deeper spiritual meaning of his fall in the Tomb, but the diagnosis was too much sun, not enough water, and food from the Daulat Hotel.

A few days later, out at Meherabad, Padri asked him how he was doing. Ken answered pathetically, "I think I'll make it."

Padri growled, "Sir, you haven't even reached the frontier."

Ken's Version:

February 7, 1973: It was morning arti, and we were singing the "Western," now "American Arti." I think we were just reaching for the high notes on "What in the worlds can I offer as mine?"

The next thing I remember was being pulled from the marble slab and being very reluctant to leave whatever very, very pleasant mental state I was in.

Then off to the hospital, as Barb described above. Sometime during the course of the afternoon Tom Decker (emergency room doctor from Florida) walked into the room. He had just arrived at the Trust Office and Adi had sent him over to see me. He gave me a quick once-over and didn't seem alarmed.

For much of the day, I had a terrific headache. Eventually the pain traveled slowly down my spine until it reached...well, as far as it could go and was expelled.

Later at Meherazad, Mani remarked that my mind was quieter. I think I noticed that myself.

I still have the X-ray proving that I have a thick skull.

A Strange Circumstance

by Arthur Trupp

My first journey to India was November '74 through January '75. I was 21 years of age and had never before traveled overseas, much less to a land as exotic as was India. In Meherabad, in the early days after my arrival, I would love simply to sit within the chamber of the little structure we call Samadhi and enjoy the exceptional proximity of the spirit of our Beloved Lord, Meher Baba. One day, during the heat of November in 1974, I was sitting in the Samadhi along with a new friend I had met on the plane coming from the United States, Steve Essley, then from Eugene, Oregon.

We are whiling our time away peacefully in the quiet of the Tomb, sitting near the marble stone which covers the crypt, when suddenly, a tremor rumbles throughout.

The ground around us shakes as if an earthquake is under us, and the Tomb itself seems to shiver while it too trembles a moment. Sometime within that moment, there is a pause of sorts in the quiet inside the Tomb, and in all this strange circumstance, *the marble slab which covers the resting place of the Dearly Beloved lifts briefly but distinctly from the head of the stone several inches off the ground, and then falls back to rest exactly from where it had risen.*

Afterward, the quiet of the Tomb grows quieter. Steve and I are each looking at the other in the wonder of what has just happened. I don't recall a single word we spoke that day after the incident, as the air around us was taut with disbelief.

Tea time came at 3 P.M. on Meherabad Hill and I remember coming into Mansari's kitchen where the chai was always tasty and the conversation friendly. I asked her to listen to our story, and she did so with great interest. And while I can't recall the details of Mansari's full response, I remember very well how concerned she remained after I'd told the story. She asked if it was okay to retell the incident to Padri and so to involve him in this too. I assented, of course.

A day or so later, Padri sought me out and asked me for my best details of what had happened. After combing over my memory of the event, as a young musician, I mentioned in my best vernacular that it felt like a drumstick was hitting a drum-head from the inside of the enclosed marble top. Padri began spouting something about the local military testing high explosives in the region. It was obvious he was not happy in the least. More to the point, his concern was all about the safeguarding of the Tomb site, its environs, and especially the actual marble, which was in his eyes never, ever to be compromised. One had to marvel at the power this man brought to action, for whatever conversation Padri had next with the forces of the military, the issue was seemingly resolved.

My Search for Forgiveness

by Evie Lindemann

This tale concerns the ways that Baba listens to our spiritual entreaties and helps us release the burdensome weight of the impediments to our spiritual growth. It also reveals my unrelenting urge to find forgiveness. I have forgotten the exact number of journeys to India it took before I felt some semblance of a re-interpreting of particular family dynamics and events without pain, without shame, and without a need for secrecy.

Each time I entered the Tomb, I remembered my father to Baba. I asked for clarity about my father's death, its meaning, and what karmic implications there were for him in committing suicide. I asked Baba to forgive him and I asked Baba to help me find forgiveness for him. I had read the spiritual literature about the debt one takes on by a decision to end one's life in a non-natural way. It did not look like a good karmic outcome for my father in this respect, and it troubled me greatly. That, and the anxiety I felt at what might happen if I told others how he had died and how I might be judged.

Not only did I feel abandoned by my father, but I also felt the taint of his life of struggle, success, depression, alcohol and desperation. Because of my background as a family therapist, and my wish to dig underneath his behavior for a deeper truth, I hoped Baba would give me some jolting *aha* that would make it all disappear. It was not to be.

Instead, dealing with my father's suicide involved numerous visits to the Tomb, dusty sandals, a choking sensation in my throat for the tears that were unshed, rapid fire thoughts that took me away from the beauty of the moment, and many private talks with Arnavaz to help settle my restless mind and wounded heart. I can still hear her soft, honeyed voice telling me: "Just give it all to Baba, dear." Then the tears spilled down my cheeks at feeling how simple it might be if I could just let go, even a little bit, into trusting that Baba would help me.

I often felt like my psyche was tied up with a tightly coiled rope, and each visit to the Samadhi wore a little bit of the fiber away until it resembled a texture bitten into by a mouse wanting material for its nest. When the rope frayed enough to separate, it was not a momentous event, not a sharp snapping of the threads, not something that startled me into a new truth. It was slow, with a rhythm of its own, and a low humming sound that accompanied it.

This extended journey revealed itself in my art work, in my writing and in letters I wrote to Dad, knowing he would never read them. I went to his graveside and read my letters aloud, with more tears, and then burned them into fine ash that I mixed with soil to nourish a young, tender house plant. I looked at photos of him in his boyhood, a shy boy with a stutter and a German accent, standing by an old car and some hay bales. I mourned with him when his baby brother died from the stick of a diaper pin that turned septic because there were no antibiotics to cure him, and when his father blamed him for problems that he did not cause. These were some of the dark threads that slowly wove their way into my consciousness as I sat in the Tomb during all those pilgrimages, like tiny bits of moisture falling on the barren lands in my psyche.

I began to notice new feelings and thoughts about Dad, about how we were so similar in some ways. About what he had been able to offer me, how he taught me to play chess and took me out to the country along the canal banks to drive his pickup when I was too young for a driver's license. About how he sided with me in an academically challenging boarding school against the fierce chill of nuns who had no understanding of adolescent girls. The freeze in my heart began to melt away slowly, over time, because I could not have taken it in a big dose. Baba knew this and did not want me to break as I took faltering steps toward forgiveness.

In the end it is said that forgiveness is more for the forgiver than the forgiven. Releasing dark memories helps to clean up the pond waters of the psyche. While this may mostly be true, I came to feel that it was also for Dad, that placing his photo on the Samadhi, and remembering him to Baba during moments of sorrow and rage, might have altered his future life course too.

Ironically, the greatest wounding in my family life, at my father's hands, was also the greatest gift. The desperation I felt after this blow that resounded deeply into my interior life catalyzed a two-year journey overland through danger, toil, fear and fascination. I lived on an

Israeli kibbutz in the Jordan Valley with bomb shelters and buildings that shook because of repeated shellings, hitchhiked across North Africa, trekked in kibbutz-made sandals across the Himalayas, ingested a great many hallucinogens in Afghanistan and India, and supplicated some unknown force for meaning on a daily basis.

And through all of this I ended up at Baba's Tomb, where Baba helped me to forgive my father, to love my father again with an innocent and playful love, resembling special moments in my childhood, and to feel grateful that I was here, and that I was Baba's, because, in the end, my father had helped me to get here.

Silence Day, July 10, 1975

by Ken Neunzig

In July of 1975 I made my first pilgrimage to Meherabad, and Meherazad, India. The experience there of Meher Baba's love and family deepened and broadened my life with Him. One event that I still don't fathom today occurred on Silence Day, July 10, the fiftieth anniversary of Baba's silence. We were, of course, all on silence, and I had bicycled from Ahmednagar to the Samadhi for the day.

I was sitting within the Tomb with one or two others, when suddenly someone was at the door beckoning us to come out. But by the time I could grasp her meaning, another one of the women mandali gestured for me to remain sitting were I was, to the right of the marble. Before I knew what was happening, Mehera in one swift unbroken motion, entered and fell upon the stone full length. Her movement seemed to contain the totality of surrender. All was thrown upon the marble marker of The Beloved.

To describe what I experienced! A thunderous, intimate yet overwhelming reverberation. It was as if simultaneously the Tomb had been hit by lightning and an earthquake had struck. So real it truly seemed external, and yet so profoundly within that I did not speak of it for many years to anyone.

As to the significance, I still can only wonder. Was it a glimpse of the union of heaven and earth, the lover and the Beloved? The breaking of the silence within?

Jai Avatar Meher Baba (written July 1997)

This Is Home

by Bob Jaeger

It was early August 1976, my last day at Meherabad. I walked up the hill to the Samadhi to say goodbye, laid my head on the cool stone at Baba's feet for a long time, then sat. I had never felt more at home than in these fleeting few weeks. So this is where I fit. This is home. I didn't want to go, but I couldn't stay. As I left the Tomb Nana Kher hugged me, and out of nowhere, taking me completely by surprise, I sobbed. I couldn't stop, but Nana held me till I did. I walked down the hill, caught the train, then one plane and another on my way back to Colorado to continue a life that would never be the same.

Service in Music

by Elaine Munson

In 1977 I took my first trip to India to visit Baba's Samadhi and His mandali. I had developed an inner communication with Baba for a few years. I arrived in Mumbai to stay at Nargis's and then proceeded by taxi across the Ghats to Pune and then Ahmednagar, Meherazad, and Meherabad, where I took a rickshaw to the foot of the railroad tracks and walked up the path to the Samadhi. I felt a great relief bowing to Baba at the Samadhi. Finally reaching the Man Who Knew Me.

I had experienced selective silence for many years and barely spoke a word when I first arrived in Meherazad. At the time I did not know it was selective silence—only knew I was painfully shy and said only about ten to fifteen words a day.

I met Mehera, Mani, Arnavoz, Eruch, Aloba, Bal Natu, Pendu, and Bhau. Arnavoz had a private meeting with me and eased my throat restriction. I was able to start talking after extreme culture shock. Mehera invited us to tea and we listened to stories about her early life in Poona. All of a sudden she snapped at me to pay attention. I was dozing off. I had a hard time understanding Mehera's accent. Blessings beyond blessings.

My next visit to Baba's Samadhi was met with a visit from Mani and Mehera at the Tomb. I had memorized a '60s song by the Youngbloods called "Get Together." I was so shy that I could barely speak and had never sung in public, but had been playing the guitar and singing for years. After arti, Baba was coaxing me, in His way, to sing for Mehera, so at the last minute I sang this song.

"Get Together"

Love is but a song to sing
Fear's the way we die
You can make the mountains ring
Or make the angels cry
Though the bird is on the wing
And you may not know why.

Chorus:
Come on people now
Smile on your brother
Everybody get together
Try to love one another
Right now.

Some may come and some may go
We shall surely pass
When the one that left us here
Returns for us at last
We are but a moment's sunlight
Fading in the grass.

Chorus x 3

If you hear the song I sing
You will understand (listen!)

You hold the key to love and fear
All in your trembling hand
Just one key unlocks them both
It's there at your command.

Chorus x 2

I said, come on people now
Smile on your brother
Everybody get together
Try to love one another
Right now.

Right now
Right now.

Mehera loved it and this opened my life to be able to speak in groups and sing in public. Still painfully shy, but more effective for service in music. Thank you Baba.

My Experiences at Samadhi

by M. Sivangeshwari,
Hyderabad, India

I visited Meherabad for the first time in my mother's company in 1978. Strangely, as soon as I got onto the train at Nampally station in Hyderabad, I simply forgot about my three children, my husband and elderly mother-in-law! Some Baba lovers on the train helped us a lot. About 1200 Baba lovers were present for the Amartithi function. There were no elaborate arrangements for the visiting pilgrims. They used to be accommodated in makeshift tents and in the Dharmashala or wherever any place was available as there were no hostels at that time .

The 1978 Amartithi was memorably and firmly etched in my memory because of two incidents which I strongly feel are out of the world experiences. I took darshan at the Beloved's Tomb. As soon as I came out of the Samadhi, a person came running towards me giving me a red rose from the Samadhi. Since I was visiting the Samadhi for the first time, I was at a loss to know what this gesture was for. He said that I should keep it safely in my almirah! (wardrobe cabinet). After the silence ended at 12.15 P.M. on 31 January and on opening my eyes, wonder of the wonders, *I saw a huge form of Baba in a white sadra, shining brilliantly and almost blindingly to the point I closed my eyes involuntarily.* When I reopened my eyes, I saw only the crowds.

Some Enchanted Evening

by Debbie Nordeen

I learned about Meher Baba in February 1976 from my cousin, Kent Rogers, who had gone to India seeking a master. He sent me a letter that said, "I found God, and I found Him for you, too." I was shocked to hear this and expressed my concerns to my family. My problem was that Kent said Meher Baba was the Ancient One, the same as Jesus, Mohammed, and others. I doubted it greatly. When Kent returned from India that spring he invited me to visit the Meher Spiritual Center and meet Adi K. Irani. I enjoyed the visit, and very much liked the people I met. I even thought, "I don't know if Meher Baba is the Avatar, but I really like His followers. Maybe I'll marry a Baba lover." I have no idea why that thought popped into my head!

Over the next few years, I read Meher Baba's discourses and was moved by them. I thought, "Could He be the Avatar? His explanations about what life is about really resonate with me, but my mind just can't get around His being called the Avatar, the same as Jesus. Maybe what I'll do is suspend judgement about that one thing, go to India, meet His close ones, and visit His Tomb; then I might get some answers."

So just before my twenty-eighth birthday in November 1979, I arrived in India. In those days most pilgrims stayed in Ahmednagar. Within a few days of my birthday I took a rickshaw to Baba's Tomb for evening arti. It was twilight and by the time arti started, it was dark. The light around the Tomb was warm and soft. There was lantern light in the Tomb and no glaring tube lights at the Sabha Mandap; a beautiful soft circle of light pervaded the Hill. Prayers started. There were only a dozen or so people present. During the prayers a stranger (to me) walked quietly into the circle of light, joining the prayers. He was handsome, wearing white pants and scarf, and even though I was supposed to be totally focused on the prayers, I couldn't help but notice him and think, "Who is that?" Well, in the next few days I met this stranger as we were cast in a play together. His name is Peter Nordeen. Talking with him, I felt like I was talking to an old friend, someone very familiar. We were married three years later.

Now get your singing hats on for the closer to this part of the love story. A little aside: when I got to Meherabad for that first visit, I had just completed touring in a Broadway musical. When people ask me how I met my husband, I tell them I first laid eyes on him at Meher Baba's Samadhi during evening arti, and I break into song: "Some enchanted evening, you may see a stranger, you may see a stranger across a crowded Tomb...."

When we became engaged several years later, Baba's Beloved Mehera told me how lucky I was to be marrying Peter, because "He can fix anything." Mehera was telling me that a talented handyman is a good catch. Hang on to him! A tag to this story is, "Once you have found him never let him go." So far, we are living happily ever after and I thank Baba and Mehera for that.

Waves of Love

by Anne Barker

In 2012, during morning arti, I sat on a wooden bench listening to the singers' voices. As I looked at the doorway to the Samadhi, I saw undulating waves of love flowing out of the Tomb washing over the people and moving beyond us. Years earlier I had seen waves of love coming from a television set as a Baba video was being shown. Later I read that Mani had mentioned in some of her writings that she saw waves of love flowing from Meher Baba.

Mehera's Sorrow

On my first trip to India in 1980, I knew that there were people called mandali, but I did not know what that meant or what their purpose was. On the first morning that I left Villoo's house to go by auto rickshaw to the Samadhi, I had no idea of what to expect as I trudged up the hill. After I bowed at the Samadhi, I turned to go back down to the waiting rickshaw. Sheryl Chapman held my arm and said, " Quick, Anne, go back inside the Samadhi, the women mandali are here!" She pulled me inside and I stood near the head of the Tomb. Then the women mandali solemnly stepped over the threshold without a whisper of sound. As Mani and the other women stood near, Mehera leaned forward with hands reaching toward Baba's Tomb. Her face was a mask of profound sorrow. She and the other women did not shed a tear. But for me, I was overwhelmed by my reaction to her visible grief, and I began to sob and sob. As it happened that day was February the 7th, which marked the seven days after Amartithi when Meher Baba's body was covered. The women mandali would come to Meherabad on that date every year to honor that sad anniversary.

The Selfless Song

In those early years, there was often some jostling for position to sing at the morning artis. Above the fray an elderly farmer dressed in traditional turban and white shirt and pants would patiently wait for an opening. Unaccompanied by musical instruments, he would stand with hands in prayer and begin to sing a Marathi arti. Without acknowledging the presence of people there, his song of deep devotion was directed solely to his Beloved. After his song, he would turn and walk back to his fields. His selfless song touched me more deeply than the sounds of those more skilled musicians. I always felt that his song was the highlight of every arti.

How to Please Him?!

by Irma Sheppard

Early in January 1981, I was in Meherabad for the first time, and as a Baba lover, I was less than a year old. Everything was new.

I was invited to arrange baskets of roses and garlands on Meher Baba's Tomb after arti one morning. It was a joyful privilege and the results of my efforts were pleasing to Nan Kher, who oversaw Samadhi activities. Basking in his compliments and pleased to have done something useful and lovely in Baba's Samadhi, I headed down the hill for breakfast.

A day or so later, baskets of flowers and garlands were again left with Nana Kher, and again he asked me if I'd like to arrange them on Baba's Tomb. "Yes, of course," I replied. In full confidence of my abilities, I set about placing the flowers and garlands to complement those that had already been put on the cloth covering the marble slab over Baba's resting place. But it all looked bulky and overburdened, so I rearranged them, handling each flower and garland with care. That attempt failed to look harmonious as well.

I was vainly trying once more when I heard the breakfast bell ring. A sense of urgency welled up as I began once more—a quiet desperation that caused me to view the flowers and garlands more as burdens than offerings of love. I took a deep breath and Baba's name, asking for

72

His help. His help came in the realization that I was facing a choice between my comfort (breakfast) and my vanity (a pleasing flower arrangement). *But how to please Him?!* Faced now with the understanding that I was helpless in my ignorance, I began to feel His presence within me and around me...*His silent questioning eyes.* I gave up trying to draw further accolades from Nana Kher, and in quiet humility placed the remaining flowers as best I could.

Having left at least one string of useless pride behind, I fled down the hill to what was left of breakfast.

Jaali

Vivian Warren and Mehera Irani, 1983

Contact

by Elaine Cox

In 1983 I took my mother, Vivian McManus Warren, on her only trip to India and Meherabad. A little back-story of my Mom here, to make this story clear:

She was born in 1915 in Verda, Louisiana into a large farming family on a large farm. It produced the staple three C's, corn, cotton and (sugar) cane. Of course it also produced everything they needed for life, and lots of hard work for herself, her sister and five brothers. So after high school she escaped home for the 'big city,' Shreveport, where she studied and became a registered nurse in 1938. She never told me how it happened, but after a few years of nursing, very interestingly she became introduced to Christian Science, an American-born religion with a very uplifting message. "God is Love" is emblazoned inside every church. She met my dad there and so I was born and raised a Christian Scientist.

Nothing could have been further from her upbringing in rural Southern Baptism. Though she had become an enlightened thinker and a seeker in her own way, it did not mean that she would be open to the concept of Meher Baba as the Christ returned! But perhaps having had her own transformation, she never argued with me and of course, I never pushed the subject.

I had heard of Baba from a close friend in New York, 1967. It didn't take long for me to see this was "IT," my HOME, my place in the universe. After sixteen years, when I had made many trips to Meherabad, suddenly Baba gave me the thought of taking my mom there to let her see that world, be in the presence of the mandali and of course perhaps get that Vibe. I didn't care so much about what she might think about it, as that she would make the contact for the rest of her lives!

She had never traveled outside of the United States. What a huge step for her—India! She didn't think too long before saying yes. She was ready for an adventure. So in summer of 1983 Mom got her first passport and she and I flew from New York to Bombay. She never seemed shocked and took it all in her stride. Of course I'd arranged for a car and driver to meet us at the airport. We rested in the Taj a night and generally had the best landing I could make for her.

At Meherabad we shared a double room at the Pilgrim Center, giving her a chance to meet "Baba people," mostly Westerners in those days, pick up on the ambiance in that lovely dining room and ... take BUCKET BATHS! And on trips to Meherazad she got to meet the mandali—Mehera and Mani, Eruch, et al. They were so sweet with her. At that point she said one day, "I think I see why you love this place."

Every morning and evening I went up the hill for arti, but she drew the line at going to a 'shrine' and waited for me to come back for the meals. Finally one morning after breakfast, she asked me to take her up the hill "to see what's there." It was the perfect time as very few would be at the Samadhi mid-morning. So she met Nana Kher, the most gracious and gentlemanly of greeters. There was only one person inside the Tomb and one waiting to go in. Mom sat on the nearest bench to the door to wait as I got in line to go inside. She only intended to watch me.

As my turn came, I was literally about to step inside, out of nowhere, Meherjee Karkaria and his son-in-law, Russi, rapidly came right up to the threshold, and since Meherjee knew me, he asked if they could go in before me, that they'd just driven from Poona and had to go directly back. Of course I said yes. It must've been some special occasion as he was carrying a jaali to lay on Baba's Tomb. A jaali is a threaded rectangular 'blanket' of flowers that covers a shrine completely and requires four people to lay down properly.

As they stepped over the threshold Meherjee motioned me to come inside with them to hold one corner of it, then turned to the unknown woman (my mom), sitting on the bench to also come inside and assist. She had no idea of what was happening or why she'd been invited in, since she didn't know what that mound of flowers in his hand was. She obediently jumped up, stepped over the threshold and took the lower right corner as it was handed to her. MOM WAS INSIDE THE SAMADHI! My heart was jumping in my chest and I was flooded with joy as we knelt down saying, "Avatar Meher Baba ki jai," placing the jaali on the Beloved's Shrine. My mom was kneeling at Baba's feet! Before I left, bowing with my forehead on Baba's Tomb, I gave thanks for this unbelievable happening: Mom had helped to adorn our Beloved inside His most sacred place.

Never in my imagination could I have even thought of such an occurrence. I had brought her there for some awareness of what Baba was or meant. But that was not to be His plan. I do not know if awareness was achieved, but this was beyond anything I had hoped for. She never talked about it with me and I was happy to leave it at that. This was a lesson for me in Baba's attention to detail and His astonishing timing, not to mention His love for us. This trip was a success beyond my wildest dreams. My job was done!

Contact was made! *For all time!*

Lucky and Good Soul

by Kolli Ramarao
Andhra Pradesh

I lost my father when I was 3 years of age. I was brought up by my mother who was uneducated but was interested in educating her children. She arranged for me to join an orphan hostel run by the Servants of India Society with the help of Local leaders. So I was educated up to Intermediate and got a job as cashier in the State Bank of India in 1973. Within a short span I was addicted to gambling even as I was active in doing good work in the bank.

In 1982, a new employee joined in our bank and he was entrusted to my department. He was a bachelor and he was also interested in playing cards. So his room became the address for gambling.

One day in January 1983, my new colleague informed me that a group of Meher Baba people were going to Meherabad and the tour period was nearly 10 days. The total fare including food and tifin was approximately Rs225 or 250. They would tour places like Hyderabad, Ajanta, Ellora and Mumbai and finally Meherabad. He asked me to join in that group. But I refused, saying that I was not interested in bhajans, that it was too short notice to apply for leave and that I had a shortage of funds—all of which were absolutely false and lies. My inner view, the truth was that I would miss gambling if I participated in that group tour.

79

When he reminded me again about the trip, I put one condition—that if he came on the trip, I would join it, thinking that he would not come. But he agreed to my condition, which was a shock to me. The next day after closing my bank work, my colleague and I approached the manager asking for sanction of leave, which I thought he would not give. To my astonishment, the manager permitted me to go, but refused leave for my colleague. I requested the manager very sincerely for sanction of his leave because he was the proposer of the trip and he knew the group members, but he refused. I tried hard to find ways to not go on this tour, but in spite of my best efforts, nothing worked. It had become inevitable for me to join the group and finally I was forcibly seated in the bus by some unknown POWER.

One of the organizers, Mr. Sanyasiraju, came and offered me a Baba badge to put it on my shirt, but I refused. When the bus reached Kovvur Mehersthan, all the passengers got down to take Meher Baba's darshan of His bronze statue. In queue, I proceeded by observing the people's actions.

While doing His darshan I bent down to touch the feet of Baba as the previous member had done, the new currency notes from my pocket fell down near the feet of Baba. Immediately I knelt to take the fallen notes. Suddenly I observed some hand signal to leave them. Then I keenly observed again but I did not find the hand. I again bent to touch the feet of Baba. As soon as I touched His feet, I was shocked and experienced an inexpressible current flowing into my body. I was losing sense and water drops were continuously flowing from my eyes. I was not in a position to stand. I came out and sat on the floor, taking the support of a wall. I stayed there for more than half an hour. But I was in a very happy mood and also surprised about this happening, which cannot be expressed in words. I boarded the bus and took the Baba badge from the person who offered it previously and put it on my shirt. That was the very first experience.

After we visited Hyderabad, Ajanta, Ellora and Mumbai, we finally reached Meherabad on 30.01.1983, and prepared for the Amartithi darshan on 31.01.1983. I was in the queue. All were singing songs and saying His Holy Namam and moving slowly towards the Samadhi. My turn came as I neared the threshold.

When I entered the Samadhi and touched His Tomb stone, I experienced the same thing that had happened at Kovvur. I lost my consciousness and was crying. I didn't know what was happening. Some people carried me out of the Samadhi to Brother Eruch, where he was sitting by the wall at Baba's Tin Cabin. Brother Eruch kept my head on his shoulder and consoling me by saying "lucky and good soul." I heard the words he was saying, but I could not understand them.

After returning from Meherabad I explained the 'happenings' to my wife, Smt Venkataratnam. Baba also gave her good understanding and she joined me in removing all the different deities' photos from my house. Generally, traditional ladies will not accept this type of shifting for adoring a new God because they are accustomed to the prevailing customs and social habits since birth.

That is the miracle of Baba in changing her and welcoming her into His fold, which gave good opportunity to both of us to attend to His works sincerely. Finally, He gave me the opportunity to understand the meaning of Brother Eruch's words, "lucky and good soul." He changed the mindset of my wife to join me unconditionally in performing His works at a later date, and He created an aversion in me towards gambling.

JAI MEHERBABA

In His Divine Love and Service.

President, AMB Vizianagaram Centre
Mobile +91 9182567613/9440398733
Email: sureshkumarkolli@gmail.com

Samadhi Embarrassment

by Jean Brunet

My story takes place back in February 1986, when I visited Meherabad for the second time with my dear friend Ruth Rosen. In those days, every month the women mandali would visit Baba's Samadhi for arti and women pilgrims would be asked to garland Baba's photo. Ruth and I were picked for this honor. So on that day all the women came in and stood watching as Ruth and I attempted to do this easy task. We stood on opposite sides of His picture with the garland in our hands and somehow, try as we would, we could not get the garland draped over His photo. When Ruth got the garland on her corner, my corner slipped off and vice versa.

After several attempts, Mehera, who stood front and center, hit her forehead with her hand and extended her arm saying, "What a simple thing!" I don't know how Ruth felt—I can only imagine, because I know I was more than embarrassed. It was a simple thing and two grown women somehow couldn't do it. No sooner did Mehera say this, than we got it—the garland draped beautifully over Baba's photo. But the damage was done and there was no do-over.

Fortunately, the very next day, I felt I was redeemed in Mehera's eyes because at afternoon tea out at Meherazad (another honor to be invited) an unusual event occurred. It happened that I was at one end of the large dining table and Mehera was sitting at the opposite end.

The tea pot was being passed around for refills and when it came to me, it was empty. I didn't say or do anything, but somehow Mehera noticed and asked for the pot to be passed to her. She immediately got up, took the pot to the kitchen to be refilled and returned, coming over to me, and poured me a second cup. Everyone was so surprised—especially me! I felt she had forgiven me for the previous day's ineptitude and all my embarrassment over the previous silly incident disappeared.

Such are the ways of Meher Baba.

Baba's Hand

by Mary Marino-Strong

In 1982, while sitting on Mehera's porch, I bemoaned that I didn't see Baba, as I'd heard that others had. Meheru, the only mandali present, replied that Baba gives us each what we need. I accepted it; what else was there to do if that's how Baba wanted it? Yet, I held out hope.

In August 1986, I told Eruch that I really wanted to see Baba. Looking into my eyes and seeming to see into the very core of me, he said, "You must want to more. You have to really, really want to." His words moved me.

That night in my room at the Pilgrim Center, I implored Baba, despite believing it inappropriate to ask Him for anything. And added that I also wanted to feel the touch of His hand. It was a big ask, and all my heart and soul went into it.

Soon after, the day the women mandali came to Baba's Tomb was upon us. Mehera, Mani, Meheru and Goher got out of the car, smiling love greetings to all. After they went into Baba's Tomb, someone waved, indicating I and a few other women standing close by should go into the Tomb as well. I didn't have to be asked twice.

Inside this most sacred of places, Mehera and the women mandali placed their garlands and flowers on the cloth Tomb cover with exquisite tenderness, as if on the very body of their Beloved. I experienced the rarified quality of their love and devotion. They murmured a bit, coordinating the laying of the garlands, all while most naturally and lovingly deferential to Baba's beloved Mehera. When they were done, we said Baba's prayers and sang the arti together. Beginning with Mehera, the women mandali each bowed at Baba's feet.

Can words describe the atmosphere, the extraordinary privilege, of offering prayers, devotion and bowing to Him with these most unique and sacred beings, all handpicked by God Himself? Throughout, I felt a tsunami of Mehera's love pouring directly to her Beloved Baba—and He receiving it and responding with a tsunami of His love for His beloved. The palpable flow of love created a texture, an intoxicating depth and breadth in the very air.

Mehera then sat on the single step to the left. Mani, nearest to Mehera, and the others arranged themselves around the marble after taking darshan. While each of the women poured out their deep love and reverence, there was a difference. Only Mehera was the beloved of the Divine Beloved, "My very breath, without whom I could not live," He had said. And Baba was there with Mehera. There was an engagement of love forces. Mehera's love was palpable. There was a continuum, from Mehera to Baba to Mehera. Seamless Love beyond what my puny Western eyes had ever felt.

Someone gestured for the small handful of us other women to take darshan. Kneeling at Baba's feet, placing my forehead on the stone floor inches away from the most pure soul on earth, being in the midst of the immensity of the strong and true love flow/pull between Baba and Mehera gave me a glimpse into a dimension of love and the sacred that is beyond words and forever altered me.

I have no recollection of leaving the Tomb. Mehera, Mani, Goher and Meheru went into the tin shed next to Baba's Tomb. By a remarkable gift of Baba, I just followed Mehera, unable to separate from that living link to God Almighty.

Inside the tin cabin, Mani held a basket of roses—large buds without stems as is done there—for Mehera to choose the very best. Mehera would lift two roses, quietly murmur to them and ask Mani which was more beautiful. After all, they were destined to grace the Lord's image. Mani in later years said Mehera would ask the roses to perk up and be beautiful for Baba, and they did.

I saw Mehera standing by a large photographic portrait of Baba, which included His left arm and hand. Mehera chose one of the two flowers and gently stroked Baba's arm in the photo, as she quietly murmured her love and adoration to Him. "Baba so beautiful," is all that was audible to our ears. The rest was only for Baba. While Mehera's enchanting sounds—much like a bird, so full, sweet and naturally flowing—spoke only to Baba, Baba's hand became living flesh. For some moments, it was alive. One rose did not stand up as the others had. Several times, Mehera placed the rose upright leaning against the glass, only to have it fall sideways each time. Mehera's murmuring stopped.

She turned to us and said, *"Baba says, even one petal given in love is enough."* She repeated it, wanting us to understand Baba had just said this. Mehera turned back to Baba's photo, lovingly seeking to place the flower upright. Her murmurs were just audible, not her words, as she carried on a conversation with her Beloved. Again, she turned to us and said: *"Baba says, even one petal given in love is enough."* She again turned to Baba's photo and allowed the rose to lie on its side.

Mehera turned and came to embrace me. As my eyes turned to her glowing personage, surprisingly, I began to gush tears like a spigot turned on full blast. I'd never been one to cry much. There wasn't anything I could do, and I didn't know why. Mehera looked at me and asked: "Is it that you are feeling Baba?" My head shook 'no' as I continued blubbering.

Then Mehera asked: "Is it because you are missing Baba?" Oh my... The gusher became more effusive now involving mucous passages as well. I found myself energetically pointing my hand up and down as if pointing to her words and nodding yes. I could not speak.

Mehera's face, so close to mine though a head shorter, looked me in the eyes and spoke. She said, *He is here. He is here with us.* Her voice had an imploring, heart searing quality. I heard her own deep longing. She turned toward the opposite wall gesturing through a window. She said

Baba has been freed from His cage. It's as if Baba had been in a cage, like a tiger, and the cage door opened, releasing Him to freedom. Then she turned back to me, the wells of her eyes had tears pooled in them. *Her aching heart.*

All left the cabin and went to Baba's gaadi. Though I was at least twenty feet from Mehera, she called me to her by name, took my hand and walked me to the gaadi to place a garland with her around Baba, in the photo. After a few more garlands were placed, Mehera and the women returned to the car and departed for Meherazad.

The other pilgrims dispersed, mostly heading to the Pilgrim Centre for lunch. It felt as though Baba had reached deep into my chest and down, way down, deeper than my physical body. I'd never felt that depth before. I had no idea what to do with myself. I walked around spacey. Sat by Baba's Samadhi for a bit. When I could sit no longer, I walked down the hill to the PC.

Shortly afterwards, a teen-aged girl, whom I knew, began to scream in agonizing pain. The feeling I'd felt in the deep beyond of my being arose through my chest, laterally to my shoulders, down my arms and into my hands. I felt an urge pulling me to use them in a healing way. Stunned, I looked at both open palms. I followed the impulse and went into the room of the young girl who lay on her bed writhing and yelling. I was drawn to sit at the foot of the bed and hold her feet silently, fervently repeating Baba's Name. It felt like a physical act of prayer. That night, I relived the entire experience, remembering every word, and seeing Mehera with a halo, her face radiant. I felt then that Baba had been there, that Mehera had stood in for Baba.

The next day at Meherazad, I told Goher what had happened. She said, "Maybe Baba has inspired you." She thought I might study some hands-on healing methods and gave me books to take to Baba's Tomb to ask Him.

In Mehera's last week on earth, I felt deeply connected to her and felt from her an inspiration to leave my career and study further, which I did. There is more to this story, but this is the crux of what transformed my life and career (from high finance to healing arts where many clients said they felt something special during bodywork; one woman said our sessions were a spiritual experience for her. It was Baba's Hand at work, certainly not mine.) The first time I returned to India after Mehera's reunion with her Beloved, I saw Baba's face in the vivid red roses covering her marble Tombstone and on the side of the Samadhi wall. A cycle completed.

Mehera: "You Should FIGHT for This Rose!"

by Hana Debbie Peterson

Here is a story involving Mehera.

On one of my trips to India in the 1980s, while at Meherabad, Mehera and the other women mandali came to the Samadhi. They gathered on the upper ledge and Mehera placed garlands and single flowers on the marble, touching them to her heart, kissing them, talking to Baba as she did.

Lucky me, I was at the center spot below, where people bow their heads, with no one in front of me. Mehera held out a flower. She was giving it to whomever would take it. I looked to my left then to my right to see if anyone was diving in for it, but no one was, so I took it and kissed it and placed in on the marble.

Then we followed Mehera and the other women mandali over to Baba's gaadi, across from Mansari's kitchen. Mehera stood on the left side and placed flowers, kissing them first, talking to Baba. Then she held out a flower for one of us to take. Again, I waited. I didn't want to be grabby and selfish. Hadn't I already been blessed by just being given a flower from Mehera to offer to Baba?

Since no one was taking it, I reached for it. As I was taking it from her, she leaned in close and looking very sternly at me, she raised her voice and said, "You should FIGHT for this rose!"

Taking Responsibility

I arrived at the Samadhi in 1986, and put my head down and did NOT feel His Love! Nothing! This had never happened before! What came up as I kept my head down on His Samadhi was that I did not own what had recently happened in my life, in my marriage. I had not taken responsibility for it.

I went off to be alone, to let myself feel, and let myself cry, and I accepted my part. When I returned the next day, all the Love I usually felt from Beloved Baba was there, even more so. I owned my part in what had happened in my marriage. Baba was happy that I had!

I Am Not Lying Down Dead

I was sitting on the upper part on the right inside the Samadhi. I was visualizing Baba's lifeless form down below. All of a sudden there was a huge WHOOSH amd I saw Baba coming up out of the crypt, sitting in a chair on top of the marble right in front of me, one leg crossed over the other, staring at me... as if to say, *I am not lying down dead!* There was humor in the whole thing! I actually laughed.

Baba Placed a Song in My Heart

by Robin Bowyer

In 1987 I was in a chaotic place in my life, feeling that my world was disintegrating as I struggled with nursing school, divorce, debt not of my making, and overwhelming depression.

The bright spot was my dear friend, Nancy Wall, who allowed me to share her home. We had planned for a year to go to India in July, but as my finances were at such a low point I realized I would have to cancel. I could not rationally assume any more debt and I had planned a budget of at least $3000 for the trip. I was extremely distressed when I talked to Nancy about it. I was struck speechless when she smiled at me, told me not to worry about anything, that she had placed everything in Baba's hands.

I was not a Baba lover at that time, but I was seized by curiosity that I could not explain—a curiosity that actually lightened my depression. I did as she said, and focused on keeping my grades up and on my work schedule. The months rolled by and Nancy wanted to give me a birthday dinner with six of my closest friends the first week in April. Although I was not in the mood for a party, I accepted, wondering what in the world I had done to find such a good friend! The afternoon of the party I came home to a house fragrant with Indian spices as Nancy had made a delicious curry. There was also a large chocolate cake decorated with birthday candles. As I opened presents after a fabulous dinner, Nancy said I must wait till last to open her gift. There was my ticket to India! I was over the moon!

We finalized our preparations for July. We had amazing adventures, punctuated by spectacular delays to the point that I had sort of given up on getting to Ahmednagar and didn't really care—everyday was joy—so much better than my life in the United States. At last we arrived. Hot and dusty, we checked into the Pilgrims Center and dropped our luggage in our room. I thought we would have tea or a rest, but Nancy turned to me with a broad smile and said "Let's go to the Samadhi!!" As we climbed up the hill, I started feeling that Something Was Afoot and I started frantically assembling my meager store of facts about Meher Baba— what would I do when I got there, would there be some ritual that I did not know and would I embarrass myself—or worse yet, Nancy? Why hadn't I asked more questions?! As we stepped up to the porch and went inside Baba's Samadhi, my anxiety was such my heart was pounding in my chest.

We stepped into the dim coolness and Nancy moved past me to the extreme left, and gestured for me to stay at the extreme right. There was no one else inside. As I settled down on the floor I looked over to Nancy for some guidance and to my amazement she seemed so far way—like the room was a block long. I closed my eyes, inhaled the perfume of the roses, and heard a voice inside me asking why I had come.

"I am afraid of God, and I would like not to be," was my answer. " I can't keep running in fear." I heard a tinkle of bells, followed by a great surge of music and voices singing in many languages, but all the same song, a song of love.

In an instant, I realized how much time I had wasted in my fear, confusion and guilt, when all the time He was there, that all religions led to Him. I was swept up in what I can only describe as His Grace. I am not sure how much time passed. When I finally rose Nancy was waiting outside for me. I held this precious experience within my heart, and told no one for some time.

I thought after this incredible journey that my life would be smoother, easier. I returned home to many challenges—cancer, resettling in another town, completing my nursing degree and starting a new and wonderful career. I was never afraid again—knowing that Baba's Love was the center of life and His music lived in my heart.

One Garland on the Tomb

by Betty Lowman

I went to India for the first time in March, 1987, and came back so blown away by Baba's love that I said to my husband Dave, "We ALL have to go!" Everybody agreed, and Baba arranged it. A year earlier, my husband had had an accident at work, injuring his neck, and, just when we needed it, a settlement check for the injury came, covering airfare for five of us (normally an impossible sum). Our two older children went a year later.

So in August 1987, we five went to India and stayed for 6 weeks. It was wonderful and terrible. Our children, ages 7, 11 and 16, experienced the incredible sweetness of the mandali. Mani charmed them. Our youngest ones made daily rounds between the frog pond by the Pilgrim Center, Jal and Dolly's three new puppies, Anjali, Akbar and Ahmed, and, the final destination, Mansari's kitchen, with her little Pomeranian, Manzil. Our two boys taught the servant boys how to play football. Our oldest, Sage, wrapped himself up in a blanket and slept on Mansari's kitchen floor with the other boys until the mosquitoes got to him.

Such a sweet time! But so difficult too. Dave was in pain, still in a neck brace. He hadn't worked in over a year and our marriage was suffering. He had some profound experiences, saw Baba in the Pilgrim Center reading room, and had a long talk with Bal, who validated his experience. Dave loved the mandali, who were so kind to him.

Goher paid special attention to him, and so sweetly gave him a small bottle of water saved from the washing of Baba's feet.

Bhau took a special interest in Dave and me. He knew we were in trouble. "Mummy and Daddy," he would say, whenever he saw us, embracing us both, saying he wanted to see lots of hugs and kisses. At one point, we took our wedding rings off, put them on the Samadhi and re-consecrated our marriage. We're still married 33 years later.

Toward the end of our visit, there was a major incident in Ahmednagar. Hindu festivities for Ganesh and the Muslim holiday Muharram coincided. There were parades and fervent celebrations in town for both groups and, when the parades ran into each other, Hindu-Muslim religious fervor boiled over and angry mobs chased each other through town. There was mayhem, including killings and injuries. Ultimately, the Army imposed martial law. There was to be no vehicle travel whatsoever in or out of Ahmednagar. We were on a bus coming back from Meherazad, and fortunately they let the bus go through to Meherabad. Tensions were very high!

Next morning, it was very quiet at Meherabad. No traffic from town. No rickshaws, no trucks, hence no deliveries of garlands for morning arti. Dave and I saw an opportunity and went out very early, picking flowers growing around Meherabad, mostly marigolds, I think. We sewed them on a single strand and brought it up to the Samadhi.

Normally in the morning there is a profusion of fragrant garlands on the Tomb: carnations, roses, tuberoses and more, all for the Beloved. But on that day, our little strand of marigolds was the only one that graced the Tomb. Its simple sweetness touched our hearts. How lucky we were to be inspired to pick flowers for Baba that day!

A Tiny Glimpse

by Claire Mataira

In September 1987, I went to the Samadhi, and it was not very busy, I got the chance to sit there near the wall for a little while, and then I got the strange sensation that even though I was there, and watching all that, I was not really there. I was not really anywhere else either; I just was not an individual, even though I could see and observe like an individual. Maybe that was a tiny glimpse of what it is like when we lose our ego-self. It was very much like Nothing!

"Mehera," by Deb Meyer

A Sign from Above

by Deborah Meyer

In the winter of 1988-89 I felt Baba's call to return to India. I had been to Meherabad and Meherazad only once before in 1978 and had met many of the mandali including Mehera, Mani, and Eruch. So I made plans to go again in the summer of 1989 with my friend, Sharon Phillips and her two daughters, Anna Lena and Kitty. I was looking forward very much to seeing Mehera again and was saddened to hear the news of her going to the Beloved in May. However, as soon as I approached Baba's Samadhi, I felt her joyous presence there. The Lover and the Beloved had been joined in a sacred union and I felt most blessed to be in this atmosphere.

As soon as I entered Baba's Samadhi, He encircled His arms around me in a profound embrace. After a timeless moment I backed away sensing that another lover needed to come forward, but Baba pulled me back for another soak in His magnificent Ocean of Oneness.

Days passed in the turmoil of His sahavas and I remembered something I wished to ask Baba about. My oldest son, Jonas, was turning nine and my youngest son Rustom was three. Jon had a demanding career in academe so I spent most of my time caring for the family, but also felt a need for other work. I asked Baba if it was His pleasure to give me a sign about what type of work this should be. I imagined seeing this sign while looking through the classifieds and then forgot my question in the intensity of the sahavas.

A few days later just after arti, while people were still singing outside the Samadhi, I felt a sensation in my heart like a beautiful bird had alighted there. At the same time Baba clearly said to me, "Do your glass work again." I mentally shook my head, not believing what was happening. At that moment I heard a lover singing the words, "A sign from above on the wings of a dove." Thus Baba confirmed to my mind what my heart was telling me.

By the term "glass work" Baba was referring to when I had worked professionally as a glass engraver in the 1970s. What drew me to study glass engraving was the ethereal beauty of engraved imagery on crystal. But serious eye problems and family responsibilities had halted this work.

Upon returning home from India, I reassembled my studio and started doing my glass engraving again, although the eye problems and lack of time due to other responsibilities have continued to surface repeatedly all these years.

When I am engraving, it is intimate time spent with Baba; sometimes inspiring when He gives me glimpses of His beauty and sometimes heartbreaking when I realize how inadequate my ability is to express those tiny glimpses.

It amazes me how the Creator of this vast and wondrous universe could take interest in the life and work of an ordinary person like me. To quote the American arti: "At Your command suns and stars give their light, what in the worlds can I offer as mine? Even my gift of love would be naught in Your sight but veiled reflection of Your love divine." Avatar Meher Baba ki jai!

A Higher Plane

by Michael Ivey

My first trip to Baba's Samadhi was in February of 1988. I had been a Baba lover since 1972, but had never had the desire to go there after initially discovering that Baba was no longer in the body. But, over the years of reading almost nothing other than Baba literature, I got the bug to go as I was enduring a divorce in the summer of 1987.

About a year previous, I had written to Mani, telling her that, after several years of reading about the lives and exploits of Baba and those around him, I had realized that most of them were still alive. I told her that they (the mandali) had become like "mythical creatures" to me. She wrote back, saying that they had never been referred to as "mythical creatures" before, but had often been called "relics."

A temporal digression: I grew up in Fort Worth, Texas, my family attending a Baptist church there, which was a huge part of my early life. Of the many Baptist/ Protestant hymns that were sung in the church, I had a favorite hymn as a child. It was/is called "Higher Ground." I don't really know why I thought of it as my favorite, since there were many good hymns to choose from, but as I later thought about it, I thought it was curious that that particular hymn contains a reference to "planes" as in planes of consciousness. The lyric from the chorus of the hymn goes:

"Lord, lift me up and let me stand
By faith on heaven's table-land
A higher plane than I have found
Lord plant my feet on higher ground."

Okay, back to 1988. I was delivered to the Meher Pilgrim Center, checked in and got squared away in my room. It was late afternoon, soon approaching the 7:00 arti at the Samadhi. I had no idea about the arti schedule at the Samadhi, but I knew I wanted to go there as soon as possible, so I walked up the hill for evening arti.

At the Samadhi, I could see that there was a line to the right of the door—I think it was about seven or eight people deep at the time—for people entering Baba's Tomb one or two at a time. We performed the arti and I got in the line to go into the Samadhi. At that time people sitting outside the door started taking turns singing devotional songs, as everyone knows who's been there.

So songs were sung as the line to go into the Samadhi progressed. I have no memory of what songs were sung, but just as I was stepping into the position of being the next person to go into the Samadhi, a tall American guy to my left, who I later learned was Ted Judson, started singing—you guessed it!—my favorite hymn from childhood, "Higher Ground!"

It took me a few seconds to realize what was happening. At first, I was surprised to hear any Christian hymn being sung at Baba's Samadhi, but then the memory of which hymn it was gradually came to me—that it was my favorite hymn as a child, the one with the reference to "planes" in the chorus!

Many years later I learned that Ted Judson had also spent his youth in a Protestant church, learning scores of devotional hymns. So had I known that at the time it might not have been such a surprise to hear him singing it. But as it happened, as I waited to go into Baba's Tomb for the very first time, it was the most compassionate touch from Baba, welcoming me Home and affirming that He had been with me all along.

At Baba's Samadhi

by Sarah McNeill

Have to say I was a 'novice' at the time (October 1988), that being the year of my first ever visit to Meherabad and I was finding everything very wacky—all the bowing down, etc. But I went eveywhere, did everything, was gradually overwhelmed and Baba took over—as He does.

In week two of my five-week stay, I was up the hill for morning arti and I left after I'd taken Baba's darshan, just to walk over to the wall and sit there for a while (singing still going on at the Samadhi and I didn't know the songs even) and while I was sitting there, these words came through my mind. I was a bit startled. I hadn't got a notebook to write anything down. I kind of went back over them again to see if I could remember, so then I had to rush down to the Pilgrim Center to write them down. Couldn't believe it really. And next day was Eruch's birthday, so I offered the poem to him as a gift. He calmly looked up and said "Baba used this idea when he talked about the Samadhi,"—or words to that effect—I cannot recall exactly how he put it. But your idea for a book of Samadhi experiences kind of jogged my memory about all this.

At Baba's Samadhi

Have you been to Meher Baba's Tomb
And sat in that reactor room
That unprotected isotope,
That core of love, forever open?
Have you seen the pilgrims there
So reckless and so unaware that
With their life tucked up their sleeve
They dare to kneel, they dare receive
By bending down to be so close—
A massive radiation dose?
And then, unthinkingly, as they
Step backwards out into the day
Irradiated—
Don't they know
That everything they touch will glow?

Vision of Mehera's Reunion with Baba

by Debjani Ray

I was sleeping when Mehera returned to her Beloved Baba. I was dreaming of travelling in a crowded rickshaw through Ahmednagar. The driver asked where I was heading and I told him, powerfully extending my arm ahead of me, "Straight to Meherabad!" As we travelled, I felt the land, the vegetation, all that surrounded us on our journey crying out in longing and pain—the trees shriveling and dying from such a great loss. Their pain was my pain and I woke up sobbing with streams rolling down my face. I have never had such a dream that made me cry upon awakening before or since.

Mehera had been diagnosed with a tumour and we all knew her time was coming. So I said a prayer to Mehera for the first time in my life and I went back to sleep. "Mehera, if I ever see you again, I want to ask you for Baba's Love." My mom later phoned me to let me know that Mehera had gone to Baba and by the following evening, she, Jayasree Ray, Karen Skronsky, Perin Jasumani and I were on a plane to India.

Mehera died on May 20th 1989, and we arrived in Ahmednagar on Monday May 24th. Four women in a rickshaw! Though the mandali weren't too pleased at first (the Pilgrim Center is closed in May due to heat and water shortage), their hearts softened and they banded together to look after us. We stayed in a hotel in Ahmednagar, travelled to Meherabad daily, and the two trustees with houses, Adi Dubash and Jal Dastoor provided ice cream and tea in the burning hot afternoons.

Before I jog ahead to my Samadhi experience, let me say a few things about Mehera. I loved her more than any person on earth, including all the other mandali. I felt she knew me and the depth of my spiritual search as no one else did. The year before, I had spent three months at Meherabad and during visits to Meherazad, she invited me to every tea with her except the last one. She took me, someone who was primarily a self-improvement oriented *Discourses* girl, and in no time at all, turned me to the path of love and devotion. For Mehera, there was nothing more beautiful than Baba's Love and she wanted those who came to her to share in His Love. She was never jealous or possessive of His Love. Her wish to please Baba was paramount and she truly wanted everyone to know what His Love was like. She would repeatedly say, "Ask Him for His Love." Nothing was as important. "Don't ask Him for anything except His Love."

On the day I had the most beautiful experience in the Samadhi, we were having tea at Jal and Dolly's house. It was hot and the afternoon siesta feeling wasn't leaving me. I looked up at a huge painting on the wall and I began to see it as the Avatar descending into Creation. I had never thought of Mehera as representing Creation before that. She was Baba's Beloved. Yet the painted image of Baba with a crown, looking down through blue-grey hazy clouds became the descent of the Avatar and the clouds were the swirling illusion of Creation. I was becoming absorbed in the painting and knowledge was coming to me.

As usual, after tea, we women went up to the Samadhi for evening arti. As I took darshan at Baba's feet, I was so sleepy that I could not lift my head up. It felt like a heavy weight was put on top and there was nothing I could do about it. Being a considerate person by nature, I was aware of the queue behind me and I was trying desperately to raise my head. I just couldn't. I was drifting in and out of sleep. So, I began to pray to Baba to help me and I was finally able to lift my head.

Luckily, everyone let me take my time. Even so, I was still barely able to keep awake. I tried to focus on the murals on the walls, to remain externally aware—that's when it began to really happen.

I have never mentioned this part to anyone before. My entrance into the vision was of the female form—the curvatures and graceful motions. I didn't understand why until I read what Baba said about the sculptures monks made in places like Ellora Caves. He said the outer depicted many erotic postures and would deter those who weren't truly interested in the deeper aspects of the spiritual. But those who don't get caught up in it, go within to behold the deities more truly. I saw those images in my vision as graceful beauty—those curves as representing creation—the feminine essence and its curvature as something I don't have words to explain. It made sense to me.

As I saw those images, all in a vibrant light blue colour, (the murals inside the Samadhi at that time were painted in brown and murky shades), I began to see the face and form of both Mehera and Baba. Oh, they were dancing, they were kissing, they were beaming with happiness. Shining and glowing with joyful delight. Everywhere I looked, there they were, holding each other, one moment this and one moment that.

I felt shy. This was private. I shouldn't be looking at Baba and Mehera kissing— mind you, not passionate kisses. Happy ones. Still, I was trying to turn away, to give them privacy, but it was happening everywhere. Wherever I looked, their faces were overlapping. One moment Mehera, next moment Baba, moving and shifting, dancing, kissing, joyful. All the murals inside Baba's Samadhi were in motion of images in bright shades of blue, white and yellow. Baba's and Mehera's faces were realistic but in painting-like shades of bright pastels.

I felt their joy uplifting me in happiness for them. I still felt like I was invading their privacy, so I came up with the idea to just focus on the wall, not at the images. I did and the whole wall became a giant face of Mehera and Baba, cheek to cheek, kissing one another. That didn't work. So, I thought, I'll focus on tiny areas of the mural wall instead. Lo and behold, Baba's and Mehera's faces became tiny little fairies, dancing and happy in the tiny areas!

By this time, I was quite awake and decided the only thing to do was get out, so I went to the side where Mehera was buried. There was just a mound of dirt on top of the ground at that time. I bowed my head at Mehera's feet and even in the dirt and stones, I saw Mehera's and Baba's joyful reunion. I was still trying to pull my sight out of this, not recognizing the worth of what was being shared with me. I was young and I didn't understand. I didn't know how to deal with it. But Baba had enormous patience with me.

Still kneeling on the ground at Mehera's feet, I looked up and saw a neem tree, where the dance of happiness continued to play on the leaves moving in the breeze. It was joyful and beautiful. I looked up at the sky, thinking that in the expansive blue the images would cease, but in the clouds the same loving faces continued to dance in happiness.

As I moved to get up, I noticed that the dance was going on even on the ground around my feet. I froze. Oh my God, what do I do? I can't step on Baba's and Mehera's faces! That would be sacrilegious. I stood there for a long while, unable to take a step. Eruch had severely instructed us to leave immediately after prayers and not to linger for singing and yet, I knew from all that Mehera had taught us about being most mindful of Baba's photos and words, that His image was precious. Obedience to Eruch won. I convinced myself that if I didn't look at the ground, it wouldn't matter. God was everywhere, what was taking place was everywhere, there was nothing I could do to change it.

I watched the dancing images on our rickshaw ride back to the hotel, I watched them in the food that I ate. At that point, Jeff Wolverton, who was at Meherabad also, noticed that I was behaving strangely and he compared me to a mast. I told him that I was seeing Baba and Mehera dancing on the food and everywhere I looked. He understood and said that I was having a spiritual experience. By that time, I too, had accepted it and I even managed to eat Baba and Mehera in the rice!

In our hotel room, I was completely mesmerized with the cracks in the walls and couldn't close my eyes. In the dark I went from visual images of Baba and Mehera to a deep state of knowledge. In the window grills, I saw the turning of Creation, its continuation, its cyclic infinity, its never-ending beautiful waves of existence. I saw and understood things of the past and the future and I was being drawn into a deep state of fore-knowledge. I began to see the mandali and mast Mohammad within imagery that was giving me unspoken knowledge from within.

I began to think, "Oh, I have to remember this so I can tell others!" Before, I had been trying to push the experience away, now I was trying to keep it. As soon as I tried to pull it to me instead of being drawn into it, it began to dissipate and I instantly lost it. This is important to know about spiritual experiences—that if you try to bring it down to your level, it seeps away. It's important to be taken into it and to trust it and to just go wherever it takes you.

When I came out of "it," the knowledge went because the mind with which I perceived it had gone. Each part had a significant meaning and the sum of the parts had a meaning of its own and any combination of parts had meaning as well. Any angle from which it could be looked at reflected Creation in deeply resonating meaning. I knew that Mehera was Creation and that the Avatar descended through her and was born of her in order for us to perceive God as Man.

I was filled with a quiet radiance.

When news got to Mani, she came and asked me about it. I remember saying to her, "It wasn't a sixth plane seeing God everywhere kind of a thing, you know. It might not have even been the planes but it was quite bright." She was tickled pink and she said, "You know, Debjani, we have heard many so-called experiences, and people sometimes make it up as they go along, each trying to outdo the other. We can never know. So I had to find out for myself. You were given a precious gift by Mehera."

She shared with me a similar experience she had of seeing Mehera in a grotto. That was so sweet. Mani was grieving very deeply, so it was most special to share with her Mehera's and Baba's happiness to make Mani happy.

A New Perspective

by Rajendra Rohanekar
Amaravati, Maharastra

I was an atheist. I developed an understanding that life is biased—antisocial and illicit behaviors of people do not always result in misery and hardship. Rather these people materialistically flourish in life, while honest and kind-hearted people mostly find themselves in unfavorable situations. God and religious practices are propaganda to exploit innocent people and it's mostly the priest class that plays a major role to do so. My principles were kindness, honesty and a life of justice. Though I was a student of engineering, I was also a voracious reader and fond of history and political science. Though I read a good number of books, I never read any spiritual or religious book.

I worked abroad for a few years. During that period I happened to read a book or two reluctantly about spirituality, which had the terms Soul, Parmatma, Yogi and told about subtle experiences and powers which highly intrigued me. My mind questioned, "Does God really exist?" In the year 1989 when I returned India, I started searching for God sincerely. It so happened I was working in the Thermal Power station in Paras, Maharastra. There were three or four Baba lovers there. One of them was my office colleague, who informed me they were planning to attend Avatar Meher Baba's Amartithi at Meherabad in January 1989 and suggested that I accompany them.

We travelled by passenger train and visited Shirdi, Sakori and landed in Meherabad on 30th afternoon around 4.30 P.M. I was introduced to Bal Natu and later my colleague gave me a short tour of Meherabad, and briefed me about Baba's life at Meherazad. On 30th January at 11 P.M. we joined the Samadhi darshan queue and I had darshan on the 31st at 5.30 A.M.

I bowed down in the Samadhi and fifteen to twenty minutes later I lost my senses and could not realize how I got prasad. As the day progressed for the next nine to ten hours, I felt weightless and felt I was floating on air. I decided to donate Rs.10 to Trust Office and to purchase few books and photos, but later completely forgot about the donation.

At a stall I purchased paan and gave a Rs. 100 note to the shopkeeper. He gave me Rs.10 less in change than was proper. I informed him of that, but he firmly said he had tendered the exact change. Had I been able to follow my instinct I would have fought and settled the score, but strangely I found myself giving in.

Later I started my return journey by passenger train. I had an exhausting three days of travel without sleep and rest, but when I reached home I felt joyful and energetic. Suddenly a thought struck in my mind—I had promised Baba a donation and the paan incident was just His reminder to me. I immediately send a money order to Meherabad and felt quite relieved.

This strange trip has given me quite a relief and a new perspective of life. The whole experience has transformed my belief system—I intellectually got convinced that God exists and He is in the Meherabad Samadhi.

Thank You, Baba.
Avatar Meher Baba ki jai!

His Anger Vanished:
Andy Muir's Story

by Keith Gunn

In the mid-1990s at a SouthEast Gathering, I met Andy Muir, famed former Sufi preceptor, whose heart was always open to all. I formed a friendship with Andy, whose activities in his later years included writing doggerel poetry and singing popular songs of the 1940s. He used to sing "How Deep is the Ocean" and I used to accompany him on guitar, and we had a lot of fun over it.

Andy explained that he wanted to go one last time to India, and I agreed to help him. At that time nearing his end of life, Andy had various urinary issues, and had lost the strength in his legs due to diabetes. He was insulin-dependent, and rather fragile. On a whim I asked Andy's friend Mary Santamore Weiss if she wanted to join the tour and in about a second she agreed to.

Eventually, helpful people in the American South put Andy and his luggage on a plane to San Francisco. He stayed at our house for the first night, and then we went on to the flight to Singapore. Andy's idea would be that we would get to Meherabad in steps, staying in Singapore for a few days and then hopping to Mumbai, staying there a few days and then on to Meherabad by cab.

Andy had three goals, one of which was to sit inside the Samadhi. All these goals were met, but the "sit in the

Samadhi" goal was related to something that had happened, he explained, on his most recent trip to Meherabad, something like a decade before.

Andy was a soft guy—kind, non-aggressive, not angry, full of love and heart quality, not coordinated or athletic. That hadn't worked out well for him while growing up in rural Western Pennsylvania in the depression. The people there expected stereotypical "real men," and that just wasn't Andy. He suffered bullying of various kinds and had quite a miserable childhood and adolescence. He carried around inside him some unexpressed anger that probably would have led to a complicated karmic scorecard come various future lifetimes.

Andy explained that he had been sitting inside the Samadhi during his previous trip when, to his surprise and enjoyment he beheld a vision of each of the persons who had wronged him, coming one by one, in through the door of the Samadhi and bowing down. As the figures in his vision bowed down one by one, his heart expressed forgiveness to each of his former tormentors, and person by person, his anger vanished and he was freed from the impressions of that time.

Andy did go sit in the Samadhi on the visit we made to Meherabad in the 1990s, but I think he felt that there was nothing to add, no further help needed, in that dimension.

We finished the trip without a hitch, and Andy went back to his house in Myrtle Beach. He died within about five months of his return. Who's to say what more was needed? He had hugged Beloved Baba in the Barn, Baba had sent His love to him at the time of the East-West Gathering and permitted him and his wife Peggy to minister to young people with whom they had formed a close bond. Lots of wonderful things had happened for Andy. Mary and I were thrilled to have helped him.

The Significance of a Gecko

by Barbara Katzenberg

I am remembering a very funny incident that occurred outside the Tomb one afternoon. I was standing nearby as Bhau was giving a tour of Meherabad to a government official. As they stopped outside the Tomb and Bhau was explaining the significance of the icons representing the world religions on the four top corners of the building, a large gecko was basking in the sun on the stones near the icons and it was not moving. The official did not think it was alive and asked Bhau what was the significance of the gecko figure on top of the Tomb. Everyone had a good laugh when the man was informed that this reptile was alive and not at all a carving on the Tomb's exterior!

The Divine Presence at the Samadhi

by Judy Stephens

I moved to Meherabad, India, as a resident in June 1990, sponsored by the Avatar Meher Baba Perpetual Public Charitable Trust. Over these many years, I have heard many accounts of pilgrims having personal experiences in and around the Samadhi. I have witnessed countless times when pilgrims would break down into tears while inside the Samadhi, sobbing uncontrollability, simply overcome by His love and intimate communication with them. I'd like to share three of my experiences.

The first experience I had took place one and a half years after my father died. He died on 28th May, 1989, only one week after Mehera went to Baba. My dad had had heart problems, so his death did not come as a surprise. I graduated from college in the first week of June. In July, my youngest daughter turned eighteen years old and went to live with her father. Then on the 1st of August I flew to India on a pilgrimage. It was while I was in India during those three weeks that I realized it was time for me to move there.

Because I had been so busy since my father died, I didn't really have time to process everything or to spend much time thinking about it. In late 1990, while I was sitting alone in the Samadhi, sitting to the right just inside the door, I was surprised by the sudden appearance of my father standing on the upper part inside the Samadhi, next to the window on Mehera's side. I could smell his cigar he always smoked. I could smell the after-shave cologne he always wore. I could feel his presence. The only thing that was missing was seeing his physical body. I was so shocked by his sudden appearance that I said out loud, "Dad!" He was there for maybe twenty seconds, then he was gone.

I think my father appeared to me inside the Samadhi so I would know he was with Baba. My brother and I had been Baba lovers since our hippie days in Haight/Ashbury district of San Francisco in the mid-sixties. All those years my dad had heard about Baba and seen His photo. I had a photo of Baba on the wall in one of the rooms in my dad's house. But I don't remember my dad ever saying anything about Baba one way or the other.

When I worked at the Trust Office in Ahmednagar on Tuesdays, at 4:00 P.M. we had tea with Eruch. At tea, the first Tuesday after my experience with my father in the Samadhi, I told Eruch and Craig Ruff what had happened. Eruch didn't say anything, but Craig said something funny: "I didn't know they allowed smoking in the Samadhi."

A second experience happened when I was on duty to give out prasad at the Samadhi on the 6:30 to 8:30 A.M. shift. When we don't have many pilgrims staying in Meherabad, after morning Arti most pilgrims are gone. When no one was around, I would sometimes sit inside the Samadhi, keeping my ear alert for sound. One time, as I was stepping backward out of the Samadhi, I crossed an invisible force field in the doorway. It was just like in the Star Trek movies! There was a force field that one passes through going in and out of the doorway of the Samadhi. I guess it is always there. But for some reason I was able to become aware of it. Often when I'm on prasad duty in the morning, standing only a few feet away, I look at the doorway of the Samadhi, and remember that force field. I have never again experienced it, but I am very aware now of its presence.

The third experience happened on Mehera's birthday—every year a special Women's Arti was held at the Samadhi around 10:00 A.M., until Meheru, the last of the women mandali, died. During that time, I collected donations from the Meherabad residents to put a long, lovely garland on Mehera's shrine. After the prayers and singing of this Birthday Arti, the women mandali, women residents, and the women pilgrims went to Mehera's shrine and put beautiful garlands on it. Then everyone went to Mani's shrine and did the same thing, continuing to Baba's Cabin Room and then the gaadi under the Tin Shed.

I always had enough donations to also buy a garland for the Samadhi, and smaller garlands for Mani and Baba's Cabin Room. Once I was about to order the garlands from a flowerwala for the birthday arti. I was standing next to the Sahah Mandap (the covered platform across from the Samadhi) where the flowerwalas sit. Suddenly I noticed a cloud of light surrounded not just the whole upper part of the Samadhi, but also a large part of the open space above it. Baba's voice spoke from within the cloud, "Do you think you might have enough to also buy a garland for the gaadi?" This was said in such a humble voice, and with such deep understanding that the decision would be completely up to me, that I was free to say yes or no. I just hadn't thought about including a garland for the gaadi.

As I write this, tears are coming to my eyes. Imagine. Just imagine. Here is the Divine Beloved, the Beloved of all creation—Beloved Baba—asking me if I might have enough to also buy a garland for His gaadi. He asked in such a humble, unexpected, and loving way, with such sweetness and kindness. My heart immediately saw that to Baba, His gaadi was important. Of course my heart melted! I immediately told Baba yes. *Yes, Baba*, I will always have enough money to include a garland for Your gaadi.

So, even up to now, whenever I buy garlands for the Samadhi, Mehera, Mani, and Baba's Cabin Room, I also include one for His gaadi.

Singing for Baba

by Cynthia Barrientos

Each year, I have been blessed with the opportunity to visit Meherabad during different months of the pilgrim season. On my first pilgrimage in November of 1994, one of the many highlights of being at the Samadhi was morning and evening arti. For many years, the Meher Pilgrim Center (MPC) and the Meher Pilgrim Retreat (MPR) were filled with Baba Lovers from around India and other countries. Many were musicians who played a variety of instruments and offered beautiful voices and songs that often invited all present to join in. As a member of the church choir, as a child I was quite comfortable and very much enjoyed singing along with others.

For many years, I was there in months that attracted Westerners and I looked forward to singing for Baba. In addition to my offering of song with others at arti, I participated in the choir for Baba's Birthdays and was in the pit chorus for one of the birthday plays. My confidence as a singer in a group was solid.

With the combination of the September 11, 2001 events and the gradual passing of the mandali, fewer and fewer international pilgrims have been visiting Meherabad. My own annual visits transitioned from February and March to June and July. What was most enjoyable to me was having lots of Westerners to sing with at arti.

A few years ago, Ted Judson and I were the only non-Indians at arti at the start of the pilgrim season in June. Every morning Ted would sing a song or two and the rest were in Marathi, Hindi or other Indian languages. One morning, Hardeep asked me to select a group song that everyone knew. After quickly flipping through a Samadhi songbook, I chose "On the Wings of a Dove" and asked him if everyone knew it. He bobbled his head and smiled with a "yes-yes." Ted started to play his guitar and sing in an octave higher than my voice could manage. Ted sounded great, I was screeching and everyone else was politely silent.

The next day, Hardeep gestured to me again, so I asked Ted to select a song. Again, the octave was too high and we were the only two singing with my voice straining to keep up.

That afternoon, I prepared myself by combing through a songbook back in my room and I practiced one in the right octave, knowing that Ted would support me with his voice and guitar.

On this third morning, I sat next to Ted, who by the way, knows literally hundreds of Baba songs and opened the songbook to "Oh Moon." He looked at me and said, "I don't know that one."

"Seriously?" I looked into the Samadhi with a questioning expression to Baba. At that moment, I realized that He was playing with me and wanted my songs to be solo without accompaniment. That had been a lifelong fear that I'd gotten to work through a few years earlier. "The Master is God" is a spiritual rendition of "The Wizard of Oz," written and directed by Randel Williams in Seattle, Washington, USA. As Glinda in a big pink glittery gown, I performed the opening solo of "Come out, come out wherever you are and meet the young lady who fell from a star," in a Seattle theater with an audience of over one hundred and twenty people. Instead of focusing on the crowd, I sang for Baba and the fear miraculously vanished.

Instead of depending upon Ted and his guitar, I knew it was time to practice *a capella*. Trudy Budd wrote three songs that were a good match for my voice range. All afternoon, I listened to her music, jotted down the lyrics on a piece of paper and practiced until I knew I could offer them to Baba at the Samadhi the next morning.

Seated in the center of the wooden bench with my feet on the colorful woven mat, I gazed straight into the Samadhi and offered my first solo song to Baba. As long as I focused on Him, my voice was strong and clear.

In addition to Trudy's songs, there are now many more that I love to offer to our Beloved Meher Baba at the Samadhi in Meherabad, India.

Avatar Meher Baba ki jai!

The Giant Teacup

by Paula Pam Wainwright

Moments remembered,
"Giant tea cup in the sky"
and the choice I made.

It was my third and last pilgrimage to India, at least to
date. I had won this trip in the Meher Baba Birthday
sweepstakes celebration in Berkeley in 1995. It took me a
year to make this journey—the pull of the world seemed
so intense, so difficult during that year. It was the grace
of His hand that invited me "home" once again, and He
plucked me out of my demanding life for three unforgettable weeks in India. I had won this great fortune. I
could never again in this life complain of not having ever
won something so grand!

It was mid-afternoon, on a beautiful February day, on
the hill in Meherabad, adjacent to the Samadhi. I had
spent a bit of time that day, on the hill, moving very
slowly it seemed, day dreaming, writing, pondering. I
was feeling very content to watch pilgrims enter and
leave His beautiful Tomb-shrine, one after the other,
drinking in the beauty and the reality of where I was. I
was aware of an occasional thought, "Wouldn't it be
wonderful if I could have the Samadhi all to myself for a
few minutes, so that I could prostrate my full body at
His feet without having to feel self-conscious?" Within a
few minutes, I was aware that the last pilgrim had left
the Samadhi and indeed I was alone, gazing at an empty

Tomb, and in touch with the most gentle invitation to meander inside with full devotion and abandon, as my heart so secretly and fervently desired.

I remember entering a bit hesitantly, and yet with delightful expectation and the urgency that I must "steal this moment" as the opportunity was rare and might never present itself to me again. I lay down at the foot of Baba's Tomb. I remember feeling the cool stone on my face, inhaling the gentle perfume of the flowers that adorned the covering of the marble slab. I do not know how long that I remained in sweetest surrender and repose.

But I do remember the loud and purposeful bell that echoed from the Pilgrim Center below to me on that hill, and I knew without a doubt that it was "time for tea." Despite the bliss I was feeling and the rare opportunity I had been given in His Tomb-shrine, alone as I had dreamed of, my mind began to drift from where I was held in sanctuary and in awe, back into the world where a "cup of chai" loomed soooo large like a "giant teacup" floating across the vast blue sky.

I became restless—the desire for that cup of tea became larger than the loveliness that held me at my Beloved's Tomb. It seemed to gain momentum minute by minute—that bell rang loudly several more times—until I found myself leaving the Samadhi and heading quickly down that hill so as to not miss my "cup of tea." I did enjoy it immensely! Had I been tested that afternoon, given the choice of His intimacy or that cup of tea? And look what had won? Look what I had chosen! Could I ever admit this, tell this story?

It is now 2020. I have not been to India since 1996, the year I won my gift to return to His home in India. Mine is a small story, but seems to have some significance for me, so I have decided to share it. If not now, when?

As I look back, I realize I've learned things, been graced with gifts beyond measure. Sometimes one may be given a gift and may not be ready to appreciate it fully. Sometimes I need to grow into things and ways of being. It is all part of my "growing in God" story. I'll always remember how Beloved Baba gifted me with these intimate moments with Him, and then offered me the sweetest cup of tea! His prasad!

Impressions from the Samadhi
Just after Mani Went to Baba

by Duncan Hurkett

In August of 1996 my ten-year-old daughter, Caitlin and I made a pilgrimage to Meherabad for the usual purposes (pay homage at the Tomb, visit with the mandali, spend time with other Baba lovers). It was her first trip there but not mine. By chance, we arrived at an auspicious time—the day after Mani went to Baba. After checking us in at the Pilgrim Center I went up the hill to the Samadhi, where Mani's body had been brought. I dedicated some flowers to her from the Seattle group and then mostly just took in the scene as more and more people arrived to pay their final respects to the Godman's sister.

After Baba's nephews, Rustom and Sohrab, arrived, the atmosphere turned intensely emotional. The twins loudly cried out in heartrending lamentation. Many others joined in the fiery outpouring of grief, and this group then took Mani's body into the Tomb for her final physical visit with her Beloved. They were there for some time with no abatement in their impassioned prayers and exhortations.

At this time, the Samadhi seemed to be emanating a very powerful energy that struck me as being like an electrical field surrounding a high voltage transfer station. This energy grew so strong that I found myself becoming alarmed by it, even though I knew there should be no reason to be afraid of Baba's Samadhi! Eventually, Mani's body was taken down the hill for cremation, where I joined many others in observing the unusual white smoke from her funeral pyre.

The next morning, Caitlin and I visited the Samadhi. After entering and bowing down at the Tomb, we moved off to the side to experience and appreciate that incomparable setting. It wasn't long before I became aware of something unusual and inexplicable. I distinctly felt what can best be described as warm (loving) waves regularly pulsing within the interior. The sensations were palpable and, although I felt certain that whatever I was feeling was outside my body, I took a moment to focus my attention on my heartbeat to be sure I wasn't mistaking it for these waves, and I wasn't.

After we left the Samadhi, I asked Caitlin if she'd noticed the same thing as I had. She hadn't, which surprised me, but then I had no idea what it was about anyway.

That afternoon, on the bus to Meherazad, I enthusiastically informed the pilgrim sitting next to me of my experience at the Samadhi. I was vividly describing the remarkable sensations I'd felt in there when Jack Small, who was sitting in front of us, turned around to comment on my story. In a clearly dismissive tone, he downplayed the newsworthiness of my experience by informing us that the pulsing in the Samadhi was merely the residual effect—the "ripples" lingering from when Mani merged in Baba's Ocean of Love. It was neither remarkable nor a unique occurrence said Jack, as it happened every time one of the mandali goes to Baba.

I felt somewhat chagrined but realized that Jack was right. I was focusing way too much on the outer traces of Baba's Love instead of on Baba Himself. It was the kind of distraction that could easily lead me astray to, perhaps, a fascination with occultism or, if nothing else, a swelled ego. Of course, that is what Baba does to inflated egos, as happened to me then, He takes the wind from their sails and knocks their owners back down to earth.

Jai Baba!

My Gift

by Terri Zee

In 1997 while in Baba's Samadhi, I heard Him say, "There's something for you on the outside back wall. Go, look."

I didn't question and promptly went out and walked around to the back wall. Was I puzzled while walking around the Samadhi? Yes. But as I walked to the center rear wall I saw my gift, on the ground, at the very center of the wall, lying about six inches out from the wall.

I had no doubt that this tiny object was my gift. None. There on the dusty ground lay a tiny seven-spiral sea-shell, less than a quarter of an inch long.

My eye was drawn to it. I didn't look around for any-thing else. I reached down to pick it up, and it is with me today. This tiny shell is a most precious gift.

When I returned home, to the United States, I found a half inch square silver prayer box that is meant to be worn on a chain and I placed the shell in the box. To protect it, I glued the latch with super glue. I wear this chain a lot!

When my grandchildren were little they would ask, "What's in the box, Gramz?" One day, when I thought they were attentive, I laid out a piece of velvet and opened the box and dropped the shell gently onto the velvet. My granddaughter, especially, was in awe. My grandson also, but his face seemed to say, "That's it?"

I told them my story and then placed the shell back in the box and superglued it once again. That was in 2008, and it hasn't been opened since.

Soon after the viewing I had a dream. I was in India, and Baba was sitting and holding darshan. There were many people approaching Him. I was watching Him from behind something that looked like a folding screen. He saw me, motioned for me to come, and I shyly and reverently approached Him. He pointed to the box around my neck and gestured for me to open it. I did and in my dream, to my horror, it had disintegrated into dust. He gestured for me to empty the dust of the tiny shell into His hands. I did, and He quickly lifted His hands and scattered the dust above my head. It fell like pixie dust all about me. And then I awoke.

I got up and gently shook the silver box close to my ear…. It rattled. And I was relieved.

Avatar Meher Baba Ki Jai.

Babysitting for Baba

by Alisa Genovese

As far back as I can remember I never had the desire to get married and have children as most did in my generation. I remember once telling my mom I didn't want to have children. Even in the late '60s my mom's disapproving reaction was still very traditional. At that young age I didn't know why I didn't feel drawn to it and that was a source of pain and confusion.

When Baba entered my life at age nineteen that reason became clear. I finally understood what had been pulling me away from the world. By my early twenties I felt certain that becoming a monastic and leaving the world was my destiny. Baba had other plans. Once I surrendered to Him, He revealed what He wanted for me, which was to go into the world, marry and have children. If I was to fully surrender, as I vowed, I had no choice but to obey.

My marriage to Robert Dreyfuss was, in hindsight, a Baba arranged marriage. It was so clear to both of us that this was going to happen. I met Robert six weeks after returning from my first trip to Meherabad where I had decided I was going to live. During that trip I had spoken to Mani about living there. She wisely counseled me to go back to the West and finish school first. I was willing to do that, feeling sure I would be back at Meherabad as a resident within two years.

But within one year of meeting Robert, I was married and pregnant with our first child. It all went so fast. Needless to say this transition was not a smooth one for me. I felt the wheel of my life was no longer in my hands. I was struggling to fully trust and surrender. Struggling to understand what following Baba meant. Of course Baba helped me. During my pregnancy with my first child I had a life changing Baba dream.

In the dream Robert and I were living in an ashram that Baba had set up. When it came time to break down the ashram, Baba went around to each one telling who was to return to the world and who was to continue on with Him. Of course Robert and I were told to return. I was crushed. As I tried desperately to hide my feelings from Baba, in His compassion He took my face in His hands and told me, somewhat sternly, "Do you think I won't be with you? I am only asking you to babysit for me." I awoke feeling such release from my mental suffering. This I could do. I was in service to Him, not as I had envisioned, it but as He willed it.

Years later that realization was made real. Baba made sure I fully understood His words to me, and His promise to be with me always. In February 1998, we were at Meherabad as a family for Baba's birthday. That trip was a turning point for me. We often went in the summer months due to the children's school schedule, so being there for Baba's birthday was extra special for us all. As an added bonus, I was also there for my birthday—the best birthday I have ever had to date. Baba showered me with love, washing away any doubts that my life wasn't also fully rooted there, and that my life in the West in no way diminished my intimacy with my Beloved.

My children, who were eight and ten at that point, were so full of Baba's love that year. My daughter, Mani, is a great teacher for me. When she was asked to join in on garlanding Baba's Samadhi and His gaadi with the women on His Birthday, she said with a sweet smile, "Mom, I love being here, but I don't have to be here to be with Baba—He's in my heart always." Ah, out of the mouth of babes—she expressed with such innocence and perfection what Baba was trying to convey to me. Let go of my attachment to the forms.

A special experience at the Samadhi was our last morning arti. It was truly magical, even as I remember it now. Mani and I went up early to help clean the Samadhi. Heather allowed Mani to clean sister Mani's Tombstone alone and it was so touching to see my sweet child, in the pre-dawn light, cleaning Mani's stone with such love, and placing flowers so gently. I will never forget the joy and gratitude in my heart as I watched her.

Josh and Robert arrived at the start of arti. We all took darshan together as a family and garlanded Baba. The kids were now so visibly bursting with Baba's Love. Ted sang a beautiful song about never leaving Baba and we all cried as we sat huddled together facing the threshold. Josh really wept. I was so touched seeing this ten-year-old boy weep real tears for his Beloved. I couldn't believe how blessed I was to have these souls in my care. Then Hughie McDonald sang "Be, Be, Be with Baba." The kids both sang out loudly. Baba was filling the children up, and filling me up even more as I witnessed this. Baba so magically assured our hearts that He was with us always.

After "Happy Trails" and more tears it was time for breakfast. I felt that familiar dread of leaving the Samadhi. Then Josh asked to stay on, saying, "I don't want breakfast— can always eat breakfast—I can't always be at the Samadhi." My heart cracked open wide. I stayed with him and we gave out prasad. We both bowed several more times and with tears we took one last bow and left arm in arm.

My children were His. I was just their babysitter as Baba told me. They not only wouldn't take me away from Baba, but rather they were bridges to an even deeper relationship to Him. I could feel the gift in what He gave me in allowing me to mother these two beautiful gemstones from His Ocean Beach. No matter where I am, He is there and I forever am in His Service.

© Chris Barker

© Chris Barker

2020

Stones Start Spinning

by Rosie Jackson

"When I see Your Face, the stones start spinning." -Rumi

Meher Baba's Samadhi is for me the spiritual hub and fulcrum of the universe: making, unmaking, adjusting all that needs to be trued. All in all, between my first visit in 1980, and my last in 2017-18, I've made sixteen pilgrimages to Meherabad, for periods of two to twelve weeks, and have spent many hours inside the crucible of the Samadhi. My internal dramas there could fill a novel. I've gone with heartbreak, depression, joy, devotion, gratitude; have fallen in love there, conceived poems and books there, left with hope, returned with more heartbreak. I've known the love and ecstasy of arti inside the Samadhi with Mehera and the women mandali; I've watched the newly born and newly deceased carried there, I've witnessed the wonder of Baba's cousin Pendu, broken and in visible anguish, as he knelt to take darshan, oblivious to his physical pain. And I've had times there of blissful solitude, relishing only the company of He who made the three worlds.

Out of all this varied experience, I would like to share two stories, which offer different examples of how God's power can manifest in this spot where He has housed Himself in human form.

***

1998 was a year of immense inner and outer turmoil for me. I lost a cherished ten-year marriage, my beautiful home in rural Somerset, a teaching post, all familiarity, and the result was unprecedented financial and emotional insecurity. On the edge of psychological breakdown, I jumped around the world like a flea looking for solace. When a trip to India in the autumn brought no relief, I flew back to the United Kingdom to spend some time with a new friend near Cambridge. Jan, a Quaker, ran a support network for prisoners on Death Row in the United States. This took the form of organising letters between people in the UK (mostly white women) and inmates (mostly black men). I did exchange a couple of letters with one prisoner, Mike, on Death Row in Florida, but when I went to a conference Jan organised in London, there was something about the motivation of the female correspondents that troubled me and I declined his invitation to join the network.

By this time, I was desperately restless again and the magnet of the Samadhi was drawing me back. Jan drove me to Heathrow, lost my laptop to thieves as I went to the loo and, as I left, handed me a handwritten letter from Mike in Florida, along with Mike's photo. Jan knew who I take Baba to be, and though he shrugged off such faith himself, he begged me to pray for Mike, whose execution date had been unexpectedly brought forward and was imminent in the next few weeks.

"Ask Meher Baba to do something," Jan pleaded. "Mike's been totally framed."

On the plane, I looked at Mike's modest photo and read his letter to me, with its laboured handwriting. Black, aged thirty-eight, he'd been in prison since he was twenty-three, mostly on Death Row, for a murder he claimed he didn't commit. He'd shared with me his pain over missing the childhood of his now teenage son, and I'd written back to say I understood, as I'd also been separated from mine. His lack of self-pity had impressed me, but had not been enough to dispel my anxiety of be-ing hooked, like many of the women in Jan's organisa-tion, by an omnipotent fantasy of making a life-saving difference.

Next day, honouring my promise to Jan, when I went for darshan I carefully placed Mike's letter, name and photo, face down, on the Samadhi. Deciding they needed to 'cook' for a while, I hid them between two Tomb cloths. I knelt before Baba, quietly told Him of Mike's situation and made an earnest prayer that He help and intervene in whatever way He felt fit. After sitting in the Samadhi a while (how lovely to be back home), I walked down the hill, returning a couple of hours later to retrieve the pa-pers and photo from a growing mound of flowers.

Because of my chronic insomnia (more on that later), I wasn't staying at the Pilgrim Centre (too noisy!), but in one of the lovely houses within a few minutes' walking distance from the Tomb. Jan was keeping in frequent touch by (landline then) telephone. I told him of my prayers, but I urged him not to expect miracles, that was not how Baba worked. And I returned to my own emotional dramas, visiting Meherazad to talk to Arnavaz about my failed marriage, largely forgetting about Mike as I indulged in my own dreams of reprieve.

A couple of weeks later, in the heat of the afternoon, the phone echoed in the villa. A bad connection, but Jan's voice was loud in its feverish excitement. "You won't believe this, Rosie. I don't believe it. In all my years of working with Death Row, it's unheard of. "

"What is?"

"Mike's been reprieved."

"You mean he's free?"

"Not free as such. That's not possible. But his death sentence has been transmuted to a life sentence."

"Wow. How did that happen?"

"First," Jan said, down the crackly line, "one of the witnesses suddenly withdrew their evidence. Then—and this is totally without precedent—the judge on the case was declared incompetent. Incredible."

I looked through the window towards neem trees masking the path to the Samadhi and felt a shiver of awe, astonishment, gratitude. "Thank you, Baba," I said. "Thank you Baba."

"What?" asked Jan.

"I left Mike's photo on Baba's Tomb. It must have worked."

Suddenly Jan's voice fell quiet. "Well, I guess it's a happy coincidence." And the line went dead.

I knew then that our connection, brief as it had been, was done. If nothing had happened, if Mike had indeed gone to the electric chair, Jan would have said this proved Baba was an impotent charlatan. But now my prayers had been answered, he turned it into a "happy coincidence." Catch 22. I walked to the Samadhi and ordered a garland of red roses to thank Baba on Mike's behalf. I never heard from him or Jan again.

***

Of course there are those, amongst Baba lovers, who look down on prayers of supplication. I am not one of them. I shamelessly pray, beg, plea, beseech, entreat. Quite likely this makes me an inferior species, but I prefer to think of it as a form of intimacy with Baba, a way of acknowledging He is the One who gives and takes, reminding Him I exist and deeply appreciate His help. In the Samadhi, this process feels intensified. There, more than anywhere, I don't hesitate to ask for help. But while my prayers for others appear to have borne fruit, my prayers for myself have a more ambiguous outcome.

As mentioned earlier, I suffer from chronic insomnia. I do not mean I sometimes have problems falling asleep, sleep lightly, or awaken too early. I mean I DO NOT SLEEP NATURALLY AT ALL. It has been a lifelong problem. Insomnia has wrecked relationships and jobs, curtailed plans, visits, activities, ruined a stay at Meherazad when I was helping to care for Arnavaz, affected my emotional health, left me wretched and wrecked. In short, it has been the bane of my life.

I've tried everything. I've pursued like the Holy Grail every solution from A-Z. Acupuncture, chi gong, cranial osteopathy, diet, exercise, healing, herbs, homeopathy, hypnotherapy, kinesiology, massage, meditation, prayer, psychotherapy, sex, supplements, tai chi, yoga. Nothing has worked. It's a question of either enduring the strain of permanent exhaustion, or managing the side effects of a variety of sleeping pills that leave me as if lobotomised.

But, bad as it is, in India it gets worse. The tablets don't work. Routines and habits I've developed at home to negotiate it are no longer there. Noises (and India is very noisy) grate. Everything feels invasive, abrasive, like chalk going up a board the wrong way. "Take it lightly," advised one seasoned Baba lover. "Shrug it off." He'd clearly not had a broken night's sleep in his life.

It all came to a head in 2017, on one of my longer stays at Meherabad. Once more avoiding the collective noise of the Pilgrim Retreat, I rented one of the garden condos. The condo was beautiful, spacious, but once more the

insomnia proved torture and though the place was rela-
tively quiet, my nerves were so on edge from not sleeping, that even the gentle swishing of a sisal broom on the
stone pathways was a nightmare. Sleeping tablets didn't
work. When I saw Bob Street for homeopathy again, he
correctly said I was too tired to sleep! I felt I was going
mad. Why did Baba, who would always solicitously
check how well His followers had slept, seem to care so
little? This might be the annihilation of the mind, but I
needed sanity. I needed unconsciousness to restore me.
Damn it, I NEEDED SLEEP!

After many days and nights of this, I could bear it no
longer. Barely able to dress for exhaustion, certainly not
bothering to comb my straggling hair, I dragged myself
the mile or so walk to the Samadhi. It was intensely hot.
I was extremely tired. The handful of Indians at the
Tomb looked young, fresh, well-dressed, perky with
their white smiles and shiny mobile phones. I waited until there was no one inside. Then I raced in, threw myself face down on the slab, indifferent to the squashed
mound of flowers, and stretched out my arms as if to
batter my way through the marble to get to Him. I was
beyond exhausted. I was frustrated. I was angry. This
had gone on for decades. I'd had enough.

"BABA!" I said out loud. "BABA! WHAT IS IT
ABOUT THE WORDS *PLEASE HELP ME WITH MY
INSOMNIA* YOU DON'T UNDERSTAND???"

And quick as lightning, as if also out loud, as if a boo-
merang was bouncing my words back to me, I heard in

an unmistakable way, with no preamble, this counter-question. "WHAT IS IT ABOUT THE WORDS *I AM GOD* **YOU** DON'T UNDERSTAND???"

There was a clear emphasis on the word "you," you don't understand, as if the pronoun was swiping me round the head with my littleness, my ignorance, my presumption, my puny insignificance. I was an ant before a giant. Didn't I realize whom I'd taken on, whom I'd challenged, whom I'd insulted? This was God. This was Almighty God. I felt more than swiped round the head. I felt annihilated.

I'd never had an experience like this in the Samadhi before. Usually, when I'd "received" what I felt were clear messages/intuitions from Baba, it was in a cossetting, loving, warm kind of way. Even when I felt He was ticking me off, it was in a knuckle-rapping, I-forgive-you, don't-do-that-again kind of way. This was entirely different. This was the fierce God of the Old Testament. This was don't-mess-with-me Jehovah. And I was shocked, silenced, stunned.

On the other hand, I was also thrilled. Because Baba was swiping me round the head as He did with the mandali when they were out of order. Because He cared. Because He wanted me to stop being stupid. Because He wanted to give me an unequivocal statement about His God-hood, and the reproach was insignificant at the side of this reassurance that He is God in human form—He made the three worlds, and how could my insomnia possibly not be known to Him. He has His reasons for everything.

A new strength entered me that day in the Samadhi. My sleep failed to improve, but since Baba's 'anger' with me, I'm no longer angry about it. I deal with it differently. I know that what Baba gave me is much more important than a bit of nightly escape into the kingdom of dreams. What He gave me was a reminder of His supreme reality: the larger, lasting Awakening that is to come.

Dr. Rosie Jackson
Frome, Somerset, UK
www.rosiejackson.org.uk
Writer & Workshop Leader

Journey of an Agnostic to the Tomb Shrine of Avatar Meher Baba.

by S. Narendra Prasad
Hyderabad

My Experience at the Samadhi

Five of us from Dehra Dun reached Meherabad on 9 July 1998. At the beginning of the monsoon season, the weather in Meherabad was superb with greenery everywhere. I felt very comfortable and experienced some unexplained familiarity, especially in Lower Meherabad. I was staying in the Dharamshala, one of the vintage buildings of early Meherabad. I walked up to the Samadhi and as I was nearing the threshold, I felt some strong upwelling of emotions, nearing breakdow. Inside the Tomb, while I was bowing down, an uncontrollable surge of tears streamed down my face—an incredible experience.

My companions offered various explanations to make me comprehend the reason, but somehow, I could not relate to these and it was a mystery. I also noticed that this was not a one-of-a-kind experience, restricted to the precincts of the Samadhi—this experience of the Samadhi stayed with me through out my journey back home! Yet, another wonderful experience was related to my meeting Muhammad, the resident mast. My friend and Baba lover, Vinod from Mumbai decided to meet the mast and strangely, he beckoned to the servant maid to bring chairs for my friend and myself. As I was narrating his journey to France, Muhammad had an incredible look, indicating that he was following what I was talking about! All in all, my conviction in Baba was so intense that all others things in life seemed have lost relevance.

Take Away

So in retrospect, what does the Samadhi experience teach me? First, the Samadhi is a beacon or a unique spiritual signpost of tremendous significance. So what do I get by visiting the Samadhi? Well, if Baba's grace is on me, it makes me a complete person—at least in a relative sense and in relation to the society that we live in. More importantly, I learn to live in harmony with the society. There are many "upsides" such as leaving behind the undesirable personality traits, which could, I hope, pave the way towards the ultimate goal of God realization!

Swept Away Into the
Silence of His Presence
at the Samadhi

by Andra Baylus

I asked my daughter, Brooke, if she wanted to go to India with me. "When?" she asked and I said, "Next week!" I called the Pilgrim Center and made reservations to arrive on August 8, 1999. We went downtown in Washington D.C. to get our passports and then to the Indian Embassy for visas. By the Grace of the Divine, we were in India for the first time one week later!

We were shown our lovely room and unpacked and then I immediately went up to the Samadhi. I sat on the bench waiting my turn to stand in front of the Samadhi. I had never folded my arms in a prayer position before and watched a few people approach the Samadhi and stand with their hands as though they were praying. I saw a man approach and say his prayer so strongly that I could feel his great love for Meher Baba.

All of a sudden, I began to slowly stand up. It wasn't my choice to do so. I felt compelled to stand up behind a woman who also was saying a prayer out loud with all of her heart. I believe her name was Rhoda. She had very dark hair and a very clear voice.

As I stood behind her, my eyes began to close and my hands very slowly began to rise into a prayer position

166

and my head began to bow forward lower and lower and lower. Then my head came up very slowly and began to move, without my direction, around and around in a circle and I felt so light and a little spacey. I moved to the inside of the Samadhi doorway and knelt down in front of the Samadhi, and my hands again began to slowly move into a prayer position. Then my head again automatically began to lower, bowing lower and lower until my forehead touched the Tombstone and I stayed in that position for a few minutes with my mind in a whirl. I felt I was in an ethereal space. I could still hear sounds but I felt as though I was completely detached from those around me and in a world of my own.

After a few minutes I got up a little disoriented and bowed as I backed out of the Samadhi. My eyes were still closed. I really did not want to open them but had to in order to step out.

When I came out of the Samadhi, I walked to the left, towards a small grassy hill and felt quite dazed and spacey. I looked down the grassy hill and saw a woman there at the foot of the hill. Feeling that I had to somehow go to that woman, I walked slowly down. Part of me was observing this behavior and yet I could not change what was happening to me. When I saw the woman, I dropped down to touch her feet. No words came from my mouth...just silence and crying. The woman put her hand on my head and uttered something that I could not understand. I got up and then walked slowly back to the Pilgrim Center room where my daughter and I were staying.

When I saw my daughter, I wanted to tell her what had happened to me, but I COULD NOT SPEAK! I tried to bring myself to speak, but words would not come! I began to write on a piece of paper, "I went to Meher Baba's Samadhi and prayed and now I cannot speak, Brooke! Please bring me back dinner from the Dining Hall because I cannot go there and not be able to speak to people. This is so awkward! "

Brooke brought me back dinner and the rest of the evening I wrote notes to communicate with her, because still no words would come. The next morning, the same thing happened. Brooke went to the Dining Hall and came back with my breakfast. At some point, I decided I could no longer stay in the room alone and ventured out on the veranda in the corner away from everyone, to cover up this awkward situation.

I was shocked when the Director of the Center came over to me and asked me how I was enjoying the Pilgrim Center. I had a piece of paper with me and a pen, and proceeded to write a response and apologized that I had been to the Samadhi and returned not being able to speak.

She said that Mani gave a directive that no one was to maintain silence on the Pilgrim Center. I explained in my note that I did not choose to maintain silence. "This is not a choice of mine," I wrote. I added that this had just happened yesterday after being at the Samadhi and that it was very awkward, that I wanted to speak but could not! She responded by saying if I wanted to remain there that would be okay, but to try to meet the pilgrims when I was able to speak again. She was very sweet.

Somehow I knew I must be silent for two full days. After that, when I wanted to speak, I finally could, effortlessly, but speaking then was awkward after being silent for so long.

I was shocked to find out from one of the pilgrims, when I explained what had happened to me in the previous days, that Meher Baba was known as the Silent Master because He did not speak for forty-four years! Somehow, for two amazing days, Beloved Baba brought me into His world for me to personally experience a different level of Being, forming an energetic bond with me that literally swept me into the Silence of His Living Presence in my heart, mind and soul. It is a moment in time that I will always remember.

Cheek to Cheek with Baba

by Jagrati Buggia

It was the latter part of 1999. I sat in my California apartment, trying to be artistic by making a collage. I had lots of old *National Geographic* magazines and quickly came up with a piece more easily than I had expected. Only once the collage was completed, did I realise that the composition of a Puja offering sheltered under neem trees, were sending me a message. It was time once more, for me to return to India. I titled the piece by writing on the back of it: "Pilgrimage."

Surprised by this revelation in my artwork, I suddenly felt a deep desire to once more journey back to Meher Baba's Samadhi. A vision emerged in my head and I found myself inside the Tomb. Instead of bowing at Baba's feet or sitting near the threshold, in my mind's eye I was kneeling off to the left side of the crypt, where Baba's head would be. I was slowly lowering my face towards the Tombstone and then very gently resting my right cheek down on the top of the marble, in the area where I thought Baba's own cheek might be. I acknowledged in that moment that I was having an intense longing to touch my cheek to Baba's. I felt quite emotional about it.

I now started consciously thinking about planning my pilgrimage, but was confronted by the fact that financial and work concerns would stand in my way. I don't remember how circumstances changed, but suddenly there was an opportunity through my employer for me to do a trip to my native Australia. In addition, I was able to find the money to secure a quick side trip to India. I remember it was all organised very rapidly, including finding a house-pet sitter, and securing a last-minute visa for India.

Finally, I arrived and presented myself at the Pilgrim Centre office in Lower Meherabad. I recall being emotionally overwhelmed, so I begged off from Heather Nadel, in order to rush up to the Tomb. I just knew I had to bow down—my first priority. It was so wonderful to be in Baba's Tomb again. I took darshan in the customary manner, by bowing at Baba's feet. I was so happy to be back in what felt like my spiritual home.

The next morning I got up before dawn in order to be one of the pilgrims allowed to help clean the Tomb, but there were too many people already there and I missed out that day. Morning arti was wonderful, of course, and I once again found myself overcome with tears as I walked down the hill afterwards. I couldn't remember ever being so overcome like this on previous visits.

As I walked back through the breezeway at the Pilgrim Centre, I noticed that a sign had been put up to let pilgrims know that it was against the rules to physically touch the marble top of Baba's Tomb. Having had that intense longing to lay my cheek down on the marble, my heart sank a bit when I read this, but at the same time I completely accepted the rule. Obeying rules in this setting was very important to me.

Later that day, I wandered up to the Samadhi. Longtime Meherabad resident Gitaram Tiwari was on watch there. He had taken a group of us to Hamirpur about a decade earlier, so it was great to see him again. I was so delighted that no one else was about and I was able to enjoy some fantastic alone time in the Tomb. I was so grateful! I knew that I couldn't lay my cheek on the marble, and decided to sweep that disappointment out of my mind.

After taking darshan, I sat outside the Tomb while an Indian gentleman entered. Suddenly he was standing right on top of Baba's crypt, yelling and gesticulating in his local language! Gitaram confronted him and eventually was able to chase him away. I assumed the man had been having some kind of mental episode.

Gitaram was extremely upset, as he apparently felt that the man had defiled Baba's Tomb by stepping all over it. He grabbed two cloths and handed me one, while motioning me into the Tomb with him. Without words (I didn't know whether he spoke English, as we had never communicated except to greet each other with "Jai Baba"), he showed me how to clean the Tomb, paying particular attention to the areas of engraved writing on the marble slab — *ETERNAL BELOVED AVATAR MEHER BABA*... Gitaram showed me how to be very careful and not to touch the actual lettering.

Suddenly, here I was, having quiet time in the Tomb, being able to clean it slowly and with meticulous care. I realised that although I had missed my chance to clean the Tomb that morning, Baba was now giving me this gift. Gitaram gently cleaned the side to Baba's right, while I worked on the left. He finished his side and was stepping out of the Tomb. I had just finished too, but suddenly there I was, kneeling down in the exact position I had been in during my wishful vision back in California.

In a split second, I knew without a doubt in my heart that Baba was giving me this opportunity! This was between Baba and me, and I quickly laid my cheek softly and gently on the cool marble over Baba's resting place, just for a moment. I immediately re-cleaned that spot after I'd had my heart's desire.

I absolutely know in my heart that Baba had granted me my wish. He was fulfilling my deep longing and made that magical moment happen, by His Grace. This is not the only time that things like this have happened with Meher Baba. What I know is that for me, Baba always gives me what I deeply, and often subconsciously, long for. All I have to do is accept and surrender. I had accepted the no-touch rule and surrendered my desire. Years later I have come to realise: that's when the magic happens.

I am slowly writing up all the little incidents with Meher Baba that are so meaningful to me. I suspect I have these experiences because Baba knows I need them. I feel I have not had very much love in this life, but I do understand that Baba loves and adores me. He lets me know by paying kind attention to the smallest of details in my life. Nothing escapes his Nazar!

Thank you, Beloved Baba, the Granter of every sincere longing. Please help me to remember You more and more, and still yet more.

Avatar Meher Baba Ki Jai!

In Baba's Samadhi

by Charles Gard'ner

Twenty years ago I had this experience over in India at Baba's Samadhi. To give you a little background....I was a '60s 'hippy' who came to America in 1968 on a boat from New Zealand. I took part in the Anti-War demonstrations, and marched for 'Black Civil Rights' down in Georgia. I was, and still am, kind of stuck in my 'liberal' mind-set.

I was going alone across the field from the Meher Pilgrim Retreat to Baba's Samadhi for arti. It was about 6:15 A.M. and I hoped to get in for darshan before the crowds gathered. As I was walking across the field I heard Baba say, "I want you to pick a really nice flower to put on my Tomb." As I walked by a tree I saw a beautiful white flower, which I plucked with a BIG grin on my face. I quickly made my way over to the Samadhi and did indeed make it to the door of the Samadhi before the crowd assembled. I was able to go straight in and bow down at the foot of His Tomb. Still grinning like a fool, I silently told Baba that I picked the flower that He asked for, and I heard Him say, "Now I want you to put it on my Tomb for Rush Limbaugh." I just started laughing—Baba is so creative. He gets me again and again! I placed in on His Tomb just laughing at the way He set me up!!

(Baba is so creative and has such a wonderful sense of humor. For those who don't know who Rush Limbaugh is—He is one of the most conservative radio talk-show hosts in America.)

***

A similar situation occurred a year or so later when I plucked another pretty flower on my way to morning arti. This time I heard Baba's voice say, "Put it on my Tomb for Donald Trump."

If Baba doesn't challenge us, then we will just sit on our butts and never move!

Birthday present:

I was born on February 29. 1948, so I only have a birthday every four years. I usually try to go to Meherabad every February to be there for Baba's birthday celebrations. I first made it there back in 1973, and have now been back around twenty-five times. A gift to me is that my own birthday comes along four days after Baba's celebration—that is, if it is a leap year—otherwise I celebrate it on the 28th, down at the Pumpkin House Orphanage.

Back in 2016 I was one of the people chosen to do repair work on the exterior of the dome of Baba's Samadhi. We were to start the work after breakfast on the morning of February 29. Hmm...my REAL birthday.

My old friend, Thom Fortson, was in charge of the project, and a group of about four of us walked across the field to the Samadhi, all of us excited about doing the repair work.

We gathered under the tin roof to get our briefing from Thom.

He explained that the first thing we needed to do was go to the very top of the dome with whisk brooms, and gently dust off the whole of the dome, from the top to the bottom all the way down. Then we were to clean the surrounding walls around the roof, and then clean off the four religious symbols on each of the four corners. Then we could start to gently wash it. I was sitting there, with a whisk broom in my hand, and as I looked around I realized that I was the only one who had one. We were not well prepared. Thom told one of the younger volunteers to run down to the tool shed at lower Meherabad and bring back a bunch of brooms. The young man took off at a run and the rest of us just sat there waiting for him.

After a while I turned to Thom and said, "Well I've got a broom—do you want me to climb up the ladder and start cleaning? I am just sitting here doing nothing." Thom looked at me, grinned and said, "Yeah, you might as well start. It might be a while before he gets back."

So I grabbed the broom, climbed up the ladder to the roof of the dome, and then started up the ladder to the top of the dome. I was all alone on the dome of the most important building in the world. I started to gently dust off the blue and gold ornament on the very top, then slowly moved down and around the dome, carefully cleaning and saying Baba's name. After a while I had dusted off the whole dome by myself. Thom called up and told me to start dusting the walls and the four religious symbols on the corners, as the young man who had gone down the hill was still nowhere to be seen.

Finally, with still no brooms yet from down the hill, I got back to work. After cleaning off the walls I turned towards the religious symbols and carefully dusted off each one, getting them all nice and clean. I got to clean off the whole of the top of the Samadhi by myself—and it was my birthday. I just stood there feeling so blessed when I heard Baba speak to me inside my heart, *"Well, what did you think of the birthday present I gave you?"*

"Baba, It was the *Best* present that I have ever been given, and thus the *BEST* birthday of my life! Thank you Baba."

***

This wonderful gift was given to me around 6:30 one morning in late February or March 1, 2018. I was staying at the MPR and would get up every morning around 6:00 and get myself washed and dressed for arti. I came out of my room and proceeded to make my way to the steps leading to the outside of the men's quarters. I looked up and there was a young German pilgrim standing at the top of the steps. He said, "You need to go out onto the path right now. There is something you must see." I shrugged my shoulders and headed on down the steps towards the path leading out to the field. When I got out there I saw an amazing sight. The sky was totally dark with only one single star visable. This one bright star was situated on the other side of the field—directly over the Samadhi. It was so brilliant. And right under the star was a 'perfect' crescent moon cradling the star. There were NO other lights in the dark sky—totally pure blackness. What was Baba up to?

Eye of the Hurricane

by Michael Morice

It was October 2000, and in nearly 30 years of coming fairly regularly on pilgrimage, I had never had what I would have called a direct experience of Baba at His Tomb. The main thing that reached sometimes into my heart was to see my fellow pilgrims going in and out, or singing and praying at arti. Just occasionally, here and there, an expression on a face, or a sense of someone's humility, moved me deeply.

Another thing I craved when I was back in England, such that the Samadhi would often be the one and only place I wanted to be, was the feeling that to be inside it was to be "in the eye of the hurricane." The one spot in the whole universe that was *real* in the deepest sense, where stillness and silence reigned, and the outside world fell away into insignificance—a great big nothing. And each time I arrived up the hill for my first visit, I would have the clearest sense that in fact, I had never been away.

My pilgrimage this time was a quickish one, a week sandwiched between two weekends including travel time. In the few days I had, I was eager to get in some 'quality time' at the Tomb whenever I could, the 'quality' being perceived as the chance to be alone in there, the one person in the whole world actually at the centre of the universe with Baba in a physical sense! To which end I aimed at the moments when pilgrims were likely to be in the Pilgrim Centre ready for lunch or taking a siesta following it. When, in the heat of the day, there was the best chance of little or no traffic at the Tomb.

On one of these pre- or post- lunch visits I found the Tomb entirely free of people and installed myself on the left hand side up against the step rising to the level of the marble stone. I had been there more than a few minutes, deeply satisfied at being alone for such a comparatively long period, when I became aware of someone's presence outside near the threshold. Or should I say I became aware of 'a presence,' because it felt as if much more than a mere person was there. There was a restrained commotion, a lot of heavy breathing, a sense of one person helping another, then the sound of someone inside and approaching the Tomb itself. This person came down with difficulty onto his knees, all the while breathing heavily, in the simplest way put his head on the cloth covering the marble for a few seconds, then started to rise to leave with the help of a companion who had run in to hold his arm. The 'presence that felt more than a mere person' was Eruch, a fact I only became aware of as he kneeled down next to me.

I recently read a description of this event in my journal from that visit, and here it is, complete with a change from present to past tense half way through, which I think must denote a switch from immediate observation to reflection after the event.

"He bows down on his knees with effort, gets up, holds up his arms with palms opened outwards, looks up and around, and breathing deeply, backs out. I feel I have been witness to a rare and significant event: Eruch's private obeisance to his beloved Boss in the Samadhi. It felt as if he were bearing an immense and immeasurable weight on his bent-over back: the work of all the years with Baba, and then the years since Baba had dropped His body. The responsibility day in day out of being available to the endless stream of pilgrims, and much much more. Perhaps he was bringing his whole life of service to the Lord, and was heaving the whole sack at Baba's feet. The atmosphere in the Tomb felt quite different in these moments from anything I had ever encountered up until then, as if a portentous meeting was taking place that allowed me to see Eruch's incalculable stature, close up. The hair on the back of my neck stood on end."

I dare say I am not the only person to have been alone with Eruch in the Tomb, but this for me felt very special. Over the years, I had been rather in awe of him, and had long ago decided he was the greatest man I knew or had ever met. I longed for a few moments with him whenever possible. Just to be noticed by him was all I asked, but mostly I became shy and rather tongue tied when I was anywhere near him. By contrast, so many of the Westerners, especially those pesky, ubiquitous North Americans, seemed so at ease with him as he laughed that infectious laugh of his and wore without demur those awful t-shirts they appeared to bring him by the suitcase load.

One thing I have come to realize ever more strongly is that Baba arranges everything if you let Him, wherever you may happen to be. How much more thrillingly must this be true when you are with Him at His HQ, the 'Centre of the Universe'—in the 'eye of the hurricane.'

So I'm pretty sure that Baba gave me this glimpse of that great soul, kneeling in humility before his Lord, as an answer to my longing to be more close to Eruch. And it was the closest I have ever come to feeling the direct presence in the Tomb of Baba Himself. Sometimes I wonder if this was the very last time that Eruch came to the Tomb to bow down. He was approaching the end of his life, and I sometimes speculate on whether this may have been his farewell. But that idea might be one vanity too far on my part.

A Dream Comes True

by Nancy Furgal

Meher Baba caught me in His net in 1984 and seventeen years later I finally lay my head at His Samadhi.

Early in 2001, I received a special dream. That morning I realized I would definitely be going to Baba's Samadhi, and soon!

In this special dream, I found myself inside the Samadhi—all was so brilliantly shining. Then I thought, "That's odd," as there was this person standing on the side whom I first recognized as Jesus, and in the same instant knew it was Baba too! The voice in my heart exclaimed, "This place is the most illuminated loving place on Earth!" When I woke up, I knew without any doubt that I must go.

Avatar Meher Baba wished His lovers to visit His Samadhi, and I am forever thankful that He called me there. I arrived in Bombay, rested a few hours at the hotel before I continued the final leg of the journey to Meherabad. I fell exhausted into bed, and when I closed my eyes there appeared a vision of Baba, smiling and gesturing with His hands in the air, sitting in front of a large crowd of people.

The next morning during the exciting hours' ride to Meherabad, I felt Baba's smile and remembered His gesture—it felt like His life jacket was wrapped around me during the diesel-filled, bumpy roads. There were so many incidents of near death misses through horrendous traffic maneuvers.

When I entered my room at Meher Pilgrim Center, there on the wall was a large photo of Baba, smiling and making that same gesture, giving His darshan to a large crowd of people at Guruprasad. I had felt His loving care calling me all the way to His Samadhi!

Up the hill to Baba's Samadhi, the path was the softest earth my feet ever felt. Every bird chirp and insect sound, every insect and leaf, plant, flower and tree on the way felt like a very soft calming symphony of Hallelujah, lifting my steps.

Entering the threshold of Baba's Samadhi, I found out that the dream was true—it was the most loving place— as I sat inside His Samadhi and felt Baba's powerful and loving embrace.

Gazing at the beautiful painting on the ceiling of a person sitting in Baba's lap, I began to feel like I was sitting in Baba's lap. The experience of love and inner peace, inspiration and Baba's loving closeness flooded my being with tremendous waves of joy. When I laid my head on Baba's Tomb, my mind felt blown out into the cosmos, with a zillion stars and galaxies that I felt were dancing in Meher Baba's song of Love. My question to Baba, "Why all the stars?" was instantaneously extinguished—my mind let go, and my heart sang out in thanks to Baba for the gift of His Samadhi.

It was inside His Samadhi that Baba let me pour out my love to Him, like never before, and in no other place did I ever feel such a loving invitation to give Baba my all. Baba's compassionate embrace shined a powerful bright spotlight on my soul, showing me that He is the One True Friend, and that He always loved me and always will. Being inside Baba's Samadhi deepened an unspeakable joy of this most wonderful Gift of Love; the God-Man as Meher Baba once lived on the Earth and lives in our hearts.

Jai Meher Baba!

Photo courtesy Homyar J. Mistry-Homz

Baby from Baba

by Anne Haug

My memory is crystal clear of the day I was sitting cross-legged in the middle seat on the left side in the Samadhi, communing with Baba for quite a while before the impression arose in me to tell Him how grateful I was that He had given me a loving marriage and family in this life (which was my only desire) and that I am now done with that desire and only want to be with Him next time.

With my eyes closed in deep concentration on His presence, there was a sudden plopping of something into my lap. Startled, my eyes opened to see this beautiful Indian baby looking up at me with large lustrous brown eyes while a diminutive young mother bowed down at Baba's feet.

As quickly as she came, she swooped the baby back up and left. I sat there slightly stunned with what had just happened. When I had had enough time to recover my equanimity, I realized that it's not up to me what I should wish for and that Baba was reminding me of that in His own inimitable—and actually rather humorous—way.

The Divine Heartbeat

by Laurent Weichberger

I was traveling with Don Stevens from England to Meherabad, during February 2005 as Don's assistant. I knew we would be at Meherabad for Baba's birthday, however we also had a tremendous amount of Baba's work, which Don wanted to complete while we were together. I mustered my courage and told him that I wanted to take Baba's birthday as a holiday from our work, that I just needed a day off. He seemed a bit surprised, but agreed. I would be free for a whole day, to do whatever I wanted.

On Baba's birthday, before sunrise, I walked in the dark towards Beloved Baba's Samadhi with Cynthia Barrientos, and Clea and David Mcneely to arrive at 5:00 A.M. for Baba's arti, (the time he was born). We sang to Baba as hundreds of people started to show up from all over the world. Eventually it was time for breakfast.

After breakfast, all I wanted to do was return to the Samadhi, so I did. As I approached I observed a tremendous queue of international pilgrims waiting for their moment with Baba. I was going to get on the line, when Janaki, the Tomb keeper of the day, saw me and said loudly, "Laurent, you have been coming here too long—come and help me!" I knew what she meant, as she had seen me coming as a pilgrim since 1988 and now, over fifteen years later, she wasn't going to treat me as a pilgrim any longer. I had no idea what she had in mind.

She explained to me what she wanted me to do. She said there were so many pilgrims on this day, that there was no way they could all have time with Baba inside the Samadhi, to bow down to Him, unless we facilitated this time. I probably scrunched up my nose and forehead as she continued, saying, "So we will have to allow people in, one at a time, and if they linger too long, tell them their time is up, and ..." Then she took me to the door of the Samadhi, and showed me.

One person was at the threshold, as a sort of gatekeeper, allowing people to go inside one at a time, and one was already inside, and they would tap the pilgrim on their back if they got lost in their love for Baba and lingered too long. Another person stood outside by the entrance to darling Mehera's grave, with the duty of not allowing the pilgrim back through the entrance, because that would cause a traffic jam. It all needed to flow and keep flowing in one direction. I was amazed, and I hated this idea. Yes, hate. And I hate almost nothing, but simply the idea of interrupting someone while they are praying inside the Samadhi was repulsive to me. And yet, I understood why she wanted to do all this—to keep the line flowing, and allow everyone to have their moment with Baba on His birthday. Hmmm. I wanted to run away.

Then, I remembered Baba had said,

> "Greater than love is obedience. Greater than obedience is surrender. All three arise out of, and remain contained in, the Ocean of divine Love."*

I felt like Baba was there with us, and He was asking me to move from my love for Him, to my obedience, and ultimately surrender. But I wasn't there yet—I just stared at Janaki.

She took me by the hand into the Samadhi, gestured for me to bow at Baba's feet, and then posted me inside the Samadhi. My new job was not to let anyone linger too long, before would I tap them on the shoulder and motion that it was time for them to depart, for the next soul to arrive. I tried to settle into this new role, and to be obedient in a happy non-resistant way. I tried to surrender to what I felt Baba was asking from me.

This went on all day, except Janaki would change up our roles. After a while, I was posted at the door of the Samadhi, and would allow people in one at a time, to stand inside on the mat on the left side, before their turn with Baba. Later I was posted on the Samadhi porch, at the entrance to Mehera's grave. After someone went to Mehera, if they tried to return to the porch, I had to stop them and gesture them to go around to the entrance to the Samadhi, not back the way they came. So, I played all these roles.

Once, I was gesturing for an Indian man who was with Mehera to go around, and not come back through the way he came, and the man was visibly confused and upset. A friend of mine, Flint Mednick, who had more experience in India than I did, was there at that moment. Watching me perform this role, he approached me and scolded me. I said, "No, Janaki told me to do this." He said, "Yes, I know that, but do it with more love." I knew exactly what he meant. So, from that point onwards, I would gesture, and stop people with a big smile, and a "Jai Baba," and redirect them with as much love as I could. It was a profound lesson and not easy, however it shifted the energy. At some point, I had a realization, or mini-vision, of this whole experience and it went like this:

Avatar Meher Baba's Samadhi at Meherabad is the heart of the universe, with each new pilgrim crossing the threshold causing a new Divine heartbeat. Our roles were just the heart valves, allowing the blood to flow— into one chamber and out another, and so on. We are Baba's divine blood flowing, in healthy ways, all day long with Him. Now I know that Baba's love for His Creation, for each one of us, and our loving Baba is truly all that matters. Thank you, Baba.

The Everything and the Nothing, by Meher Baba, p. 5.

Go Straight Home

by Barb Jackson

When I first approached the Tomb of Meher Baba in March of 2006, my heart was racing and all I could think of was to get to the top of the hill and into Baba's Tomb-shrine! First trip ever to India, my friend and I had been delayed in Bangkok due to not having our visas at all (who would come without visas? Baba surely put the veil over our eyes). There is an entire story of how Baba tried to maneuver the trip to show me that we should go home DIRECTLY after seeing Him, and do our visiting beforehand.

I entered an empty area outside the Tomb with exception of an obviously veteran Baba lover who was guarding/supervising the Tomb. I can't remember her name, but she told me after I emerged, tears on my face, that I should cover my shoulders and that my heart's longing had brought me here. This helped me to regain my grounding after the emotionally-charged visit inside Baba's Tomb. My heart was now complete and I was ready to stay another ten days in a rental at the bottom of the hill, due to coming the day after the Meher Retreat Center closed for the season.

We were invited to visit Bhau and stayed three hours with him; in those days he was still very animated and speaking well. Such an amazing visit. I changed my airline tickets going back to Bangkok, and Baba made sure that visit soured terribly as a good lesson for me never to forget to go directly home after visiting Him. On the flight back to the United States, it dawned on me how Baba had worked to give me a never-to-forget inner experience to obey His order in going home directly! Baba is so Real, internal, and loving in His ways that I cannot express this all in writing.

The One Without A Second

by Barbara A. Roberts

In July 2006, I went on my seventh pilgrimage to Meherabad. While there, I mentioned to a friend that I had never experienced anything at the Samadhi. (On each journey, I had been drawn to Baba's Home for the conversations with His Companions.) She looked into the distance and replied that I would probably be overwhelmed by what is contained in the Little House on The Hill.

A few days later, I found myself volunteering to be the tour guide to the Ellora Caves for a family from Taiwan. They had heard of Baba a scant six months before. Both the husband and his wife were Buddhist meditators. However, the man especially, had hit a wall. Buddha had turned to stone and was crumbling.

His teacher suggested he conduct a spiritual search on the internet. He came upon a Baba website written in Chinese.

It seemed as though Baba's Name and Face were illuminated. Search over. He immediately contacted the designer of the website, a Baba lover born in China and living in Australia. She agreed to escort the family to Meherabad. We became instant friends, as often happens with Baba.

Their traveling companion had left to go back to Australia. They wished to explore the Ellora caves, and I leapt at the chance to visit there again. I had made the trip several times in the past, including one with Eruch. Each time, I had been magnetically drawn to Cave Number 10, which contains a very tall statue of Maitreya Buddha. This is where Baba had said to Mani, "*I am Buddha.*"

When we got to Ellora, I led everyone directly to the Buddhist Cave. Both the man and I became transfixed at the feet of Buddha. My mind emptied and my heart filled.

After reluctantly pulling myself away, we capped off a very full day by going to evening arti in Meherabad. Standing in line, waiting to go into Baba's Samadhi, I placed my hand on one of the basalt stones. From this crystal-laden volcanic rock, I felt a homeopathic dose of the same powerful energy that I had perceived at Elora. So it was, I understood why Baba shields me from His True Self most of the time.

I am reminded of the first line of a song that Billy Goodrum wrote as he was leaving the Samadhi—

> I don't want to go. I want to feel the beating of Your Heart.

In the Hearts of My Lovers

As I was preparing to embark on my third pilgrimage to Meherabad, I had a dream that I was at the Samadhi. Baba was there, but He was dressed as the Pope. He was at the head of a formal procession, and we pilgrims were lined up behind Him, also in white robes.

Before we began marching, someone gave me a stuffed toy monkey, "Baba Monkey," and indicated that it was my solemn duty to carry this plaything into the Samadhi.

While focused on this task, I caught a glimpse of a table to the side, where my so-called non-Baba-lover friends and relatives were sitting, including a favorite aunt, who was a person of deep spiritual conviction and devotion to Jesus.

I thought, "I have no time for them, because I am responsible for this precious cargo," (which was actually a bit of synthetic fluff...)

When we reached the Threshold, the setting changed to my childhood church. I had been expecting a grand spiritual experience. Instead, I heard a Voice—

I am not here. I am in the hearts of My lovers.
My Center is the heart of every lover.

"Every lover with a heart who loves Baba is a center."
  ~Meher Baba at the Meher Center, 1956

My Parents' Experience
at Baba's Samadhi

by Deepthi Koruprolu
Andra Pradesh

My parents were holding Baba's daaman since 1985. Every year they used to visit Meherabad. Similarly, they happened to visit Meherabad in 2009 too.

My mom finished her Samadhi darshan and was sitting in the space outside Samadhi. My father went for Samadhi darshan and while coming out of the Samadhi room, it seems he felt that "..it would have been great if we would have offered flowers, but no one is here today, to sell them." In a matter of few minutes, a person appeared before him, offered him a garland and told him to offer it to Baba. He also told him, "Your wife is sitting over there—call her also!"

They went in happily, offered the garland and came back to thank the man, but to their surprise there wasn't any sign of that man again! They were overwhelmed with joy and thought it was a small sign of Baba showing them that He listens to each and every small wish of His lovers.

In the same visit they had another experience.

The children of our family playfully stepped on the threshold (floor jamb) of Samadhi's door frame. (Doing so is considered to be inauspicious as per Hindu customs.) My parents hence felt bad about it. Next day, early in the morning, while my parents were cleaning inside the Samadhi room, all the children were seated outside. A lady came and told them, "Children, go get up and clean the doors and doorframe."

This was another magical experience for them!

My Experience Near Samadhi

by Deepthi Koruprolu

Before I share my experience, I must give a brief introduction about myself.

My parents were holding Meher Baba's daaman since my
childhood. As a girl, I used to follow them to Meher
Baba's center quite a few times. Every Sunday in Tade-
palligudem, AndraPradesh, a Sahavas program used to be
conducted. It would consist of bhajans, followed by the
center's president's speech on Baba and His teachings.
Doing so I only used to understand very little about the
inner meaning hidden in songs, stories, examples quoted
during speeches and also a few of Baba's sayings like
"Real Happiness Lies in Making Others Happy," etc.

Actually, even till recent times I haven't known much
about Baba, except blindly holding on to Him. It's been
eleven years since I got married and didn't get a chance
to visit Meherabad all these years. Recently we moved to
Pune after staying abroad, and visited Meherabad last
month.

As we were walking up the hill towards the Samadhi, I
kept thinking that it would have been great if some
knowledgeable person had accompanied us, so that he
could tell us everything in and about the Samadhi and its
premises, as I didn't know much and also hoped that my
hubby could get to know more about Baba.

With the same thought, we had Baba's darshan in His Samadhi and came out. We were standing in the shade holding the brochure that I had picked up in Lower Meherabad. It contained all important places to be seen. Just then a person who was sitting there, asked me what paper it was and upon showing it to him, he said, "This isn't needed. Come, I will guide you guys throughout the place!" He explained about Baba's Samadhi, Mandali Samadhi, Baba's kitchen, reading hall, prayer room, room where the seven-colored flag was designed, paintings made by one of Baba's blind disciples and many other things in detail and also enlightened us about BELOVED BABA Himself, that too in our native language, Telugu.

I was very happy that Baba heard me and sent a messenger to let us know a little about Him.

Jai Baba

Visual Phenomenon

by William Byars

I have one experience to relate which happened in October or early November of 2010, during a stay at Meherabad that was mostly dedicated to visiting Baba's Samadhi.

One day while participating in Baba's prayers at arti, with eyes closed, I realized I was seeing what appeared to be dimly lit colored dots throughout most of my visual field. The dots were moving slowly away from me, at a perfectly constant rate of motion, toward a central focal point at infinity. They were arranged in neatly formed rows. I saw them on at least two or three occasions at the Samadhi during that stay. They were subtle enough in "substance" to make me wonder if this visual phenomenon might be something that had been accessible to me all along, if only I closed my eyes and were looking for them. However, I had never noticed them before and have not been able to find them since.

Being human, I had to try to understand and explain the experience. The best I've been able to do is to see the colored dots as representing sanskaras that Baba was pulling away from me. In recent years I've used this image during meditation to offer my sanskaras to Baba. Sometimes at a church service or other group setting, I've used the image in a collective mode to visualize sanskaras going out from the entire group.

I don't expect the experience to repeat itself during my next visit to Meherabad, but if it does I will accept it as a gift from beloved Baba.

The Disobedience Trail

by Karl Moeller

In August 2010, at the end of an exhausting three-week 'Beads on One String' pilgrimage all around India led by Don Stevens, we ended in Meherabad at the Meher Pilgrim Retreat. I'd had some recovery days, shuffling around, sleeping late, visiting, enjoying the food in the MPR. What I hadn't been doing was walking across the fields and taking Baba's darshan. Why? Because I was engaged in a childish tit-for-tat with the One whom I was then calling the "Great Withholder."

There were two paths between the new Pilgrim Retreat and Baba's Tomb—the 'official,' roundabout marked trail, and the other, more direct path across the fields, called by many pilgrims the "Disobedience Trail," because this land was then owned by a farmer and we weren't supposed to cross it.

Time after time I'd laid my head on the cool marble of Baba's Tomb, waiting for an awakening, some kind of response from Him...nothing. So that afternoon I was gonna have it out with Baba.

Striding across the fields on the Disobedience Trail, I had a loud argument in my head with God. I told Him He was the Lord of Creation, would it be too much trouble to just give me *some* kind of response there in the Tomb? I was not asking for Realization, just a sense of someone Real responding to my plea and presence. I admitted to myself with a sly smile, if He *did* give me some unmistakable message from within the Tomb, I'd secretly lord it over others, this being evidence of my true spiritual status.

All walks come to an end. In mid-afternoon the Tomb was almost deserted. I had plenty of time grinding my knees and resting my forehead on the stone, waiting and waiting. With a disgusted grunt I rose and backed out, got my prasad, walked over to the mandap and sat on its edge, glaring at the Tomb and at Baba in general. My thoughts were dark.

Moments after I seated myself, one of the hill dogs ran over, tail wagging, pushing his head at my knees. I'd seen these hill dogs before. I knew which ones were cared for and how to recognize a stranger. This one jumped up onto the mandap and snuggled right up against my right leg and side, while I scratched his ears, bemused. And here came another one, a cream-colored hill dog, also nosing for pets, and this one jumped up and settled down on my other side.

All of a sudden, I was a loving dog sandwich. Baba is, above all, a practical Avatar. What's available and on hand? What would give me a glimmer? First and last time they ever noticed me. I looked at the dogs, the trees, Baba's Tomb, at the sky, and said, *"Dogs, Baba? Dogs!?!?"* But now laughing and smiling.

Light of the Lord

by Alan Talbot

I. In the Beginning

At age eleven, I was obligated to attend Saturday Syna-gogue services from 10:00 A.M. to noon. The only re-deeming feature here was the magnetism of the Rabbi, Arthur Rosenbaum, a passionate man, filled with a deep sense of justice that unconsciously affected my heart. Only now do I realize the effect he had on my life. I re-call from about 1959 the final prayer of the service and realized the significance of that prayer, which rested latently in my subconscious until 2013. The prayer and its origins in the Bible is noted below:

> *Blessed may you be in your coming in and blessed may you be in your going out. Deuteronomy 286.*
> *May the Lord bless you and keep you. Number 6:24 – 26*
> *May the Lord make His face to shine light upon you and be gracious unto you.*
> *May the Lord lift up His countenance unto you and give you peace.*
> *This day, now and forevermore. Psalms 121:8.*

II. 2010

Beginning in 2007, my wife Karen, a community college teacher, and I started going to India during her winter break until the New Year. In 2010, we arrived as usual, on the 12th or 13th. About two days later, I was at morning arti. I was seated on the benches on the right side of the Tomb (if facing the Tomb).

Suddenly, and for no apparent reason, the people across from me appeared as pure light. I could not distinguish whether an individualized soul was a man or woman, Western, Indian or Iranian, tall or short, etc. The only differentiation was the quantity and quality of light that shone. It is not easy to describe such measurement but the quantity of light could be perhaps 50% and the quality 25%. While this appears somewhat subjective, I was able to discern the diversity of the souls before me. I was amazed, and I stared at the mass of light before me for some time. It was perhaps 6:20 A.M.

After some time, I decided to turn my head left, to see if those souls on the benches facing the Tomb were also light. They were. In fact, everyone at the Samadhi was light. It was further very clear that no one else 'saw' what I was seeing. They were all unconscious of this presentation.

Again, suddenly, all the light of the individual souls transferred as a stream to the area before the threshold of the Tomb. In other words, the light became a mass of collective light and increased in intensity in quantity and quality. It was awesome and magnificent, beyond mere words.

This light continued for a time. Linear time was completely lost, although I realized that the arti would eventually occur.

Suddenly, and without forewarning, Light poured forth from the Samadhi. This Light was pure, unadulterated, constant and beyond imagination. The stream was unequalled. It was Love itself, which was Light, from God Himself. This Light immediately integrated with the light of the individualized souls before the threshold. The collective light became enraptured as God's light permeated its "being." I can only imagine the expression on my face. My entire consciousness was His Light; yet I was separate from His Light—an observer only. After some time, the Light of the Lord receded into the Samadhi. The collective light remained at the threshold, and then suddenly, it too receded to the individuals' souls. But now the quality and quantity of the Light of the individual souls was magnified by at least two. The Lord's Light had dramatically increased the love of the people at the arti.

At this point, it was about 6:50 A.M. The arti was to begin shortly, and I wondered whether I would be able to perform, and more, what would happen thereafter? Remarkably, I performed the entire arti, without a hitch, but then I was to return to the Meher Pilgrim Retreat with Karen. How would I function? Would I see only Light?

Upon returning to the MPR, I was able to dual-task. I was able to act 'normally' and hold a conversation and yet, concurrently, see the Light of people and creatures. I saw that local farmers had lesser Light than the Baba people and that dogs' Light was greater than that of cattle. Quite a show.

I realized I would not be able to fully reflect on the morning until the 2 – 4 P.M. rest break. I waited patiently, still able to dual-task. After lunch, I returned to my single room and reflected upon the day's events. I had no answer to the cause of the experience or its continuation. I decided it all was Baba's will, and I would let it transpire as He wished. I wondered later before falling asleep, if the Light would dissipate. It did not. The second morning, I again went to the arti.

On the second day, the entire sequence occurred as before. There was one exception. On this occasion, I was involved. When the individual souls projected their Light onto the area before the threshold, suddenly and without warning, I also joined. I was no longer a spectator, but a participant. I felt my heart open and the inner Light pour forth. It was bliss. All my sight was this Light.

Now rather than seeing with the two eyes of my head, I saw solely with the eye of my heart. I had never known that the heart had an eye. This eye saw straight into the hearts of others. It bypassed the mind and was unconcerned with so called material reason. It was clear that the mind was subject to thoughts, ideas, disputes, which clouded the heart. The heart was unclouded and existed on Love alone.

As I was absorbing all this, again the stream of pure Light poured forth from the Tomb. The collective Light (of which I was now a part) was overcome by the "madness" of pure bliss. No words exist to properly convey the experience. As I was at the threshold, I could watch God's Light pour forth. As the day before, God's Light remained for a time and then receded. The collective Light thereafter receded. I was beyond joy.

Somehow, again, I performed the arti, and returned to the MPR by dual-tasking. I decided not to discuss this with anyone. It was too unbelievable.

And so it was throughout our stay, that I was able to dual-task. I wondered whether I would be able to "read" the hearts of people when I returned home. Nearly two weeks later and upon entering the plane to return home, I completely forgot the entire episode of God's Light. It was as if Baba placed a selective amnesia on my mind. I recalled everything else about the trip but this. And so it went.

III. 2011

Karen and I again returned in mid-December 2011. This trip would be different. There were to be many Westerners on this trip.

Within a couple of days, the entire sequence reoccurred. At once, I remembered that I had forgotten the sequence from 2010. The memories rushed into my mind. I had to laugh at my "amnesia." In any event, 2011 proved to be as inspiring as 2010. At times, I would track to see who was at the arti (mornings were more productive than the evenings), so I could know who I was seeing as Light. It seemed harmless fun. I wondered whether I would remember these episodes when I returned home or suffer the "amnesia" of 2010. However, this time, I had total recall of both years.

IV. And in the End

I have had no recurrences of these experiences since I left India in 2011. I do have a vivid memory of what transpired and the remarkable beauty involved. I recognize whatever words I use, or however articulate I might be, I cannot properly communicate the depth and glory of these experiences. Whatever words I could add or subtract would be of no value.

When I first heard the words both in Hebrew and in English, "May the Lord make His face to shine light upon you and be gracious unto you," I was perhaps nine. I was sixty-four in 2010, and thus, for fifty-five years I unconsciously held these words. Now these words have come true. Why Baba blessed me, I cannot say. But then, He also said, "Understanding has no meaning; only love has meaning."

The eye of the heart, which knows only love and the Light of Love, is real and a true gift from the Master to the disciple.

This story appeared in it original form in the April 2016 issue of *Lovestreet Breezes*, #8.

"We Can Never Be Separated"

by Melinda Abeles

I was sitting on the pandal beside the Samadhi, reflecting on the most profound experience of my life. It was mid-February 2011, a few days before Baba's birthday celebration. This was my first trip to India, and a few days before, I had laid my head down on Baba's Tomb for the first time.

I had arrived at Meherabad in the afternoon, about teatime, greeted by that amazing painting of Baba above the door of the dining hall that almost sent me to the floor in tears. After settling into my room and having tea, it was time. I had an appointment with God.

All my life had led me to this moment, and it felt like a long convoluted line of dominoes that began at Mt. Zion Hospital in San Francisco at the moment of my first breath this time. He had now flicked this first tile with His index finger, and they were falling fast.

With my red sandals and wet scarves around my head, covering the red rose clip in my hair, I followed the path across the barren fields of India, towards and through the living forest of flowering bushes and trees. I cannot explain the feeling other than I felt like a Prisoner Of War who had been in exile for fifty-five years, who was finally released to come home.

As I passed other pilgrims on the path, the only words we spoke in whispers were, "Jai Baba, Jai Baba," eyes meeting in acknowledgement. Onward my feet stepped as the dominoes were falling just behind me. The closer I came to the Samadhi, the closer and faster they fell.

Suddenly, in disbelief, I saw the Samadhi there. I placed myself at the end of the queue as the tears of unbelievable release and relief began. Someone beautiful in front of me heard my sniffling and handed me some tissues which I had forgotten to bring, and slowly I moved forward towards the end of the long road home.

My turn came, and a bit confused with unknown formalities, I stepped onto and over the threshold, leaving a dusty footprint behind. Each breath of my life had led to this moment. The last domino was falling as I walked forward and kneeled and placed my forehead onto the edge of the marble. I was immediately pulled out of my body into the universe of stars. I was formless and merged and I knew beyond any shadow of doubt that every soul in the universe was right behind me. Every soul on Earth and everywhere, was on their way Home.

So here is the drawing of that experience, done one morning a few days later on the pandal next to the Samadhi. It expresses that moment in the best way I know how, as only a picture can. As I was drawing, a group of shining young boys from the Meher English School came to watch. I gave them all pieces of paper from my book and offered them use of my pencils. They were thrilled at the opportunity to draw the Samadhi in their own way. I was way more thrilled than they were!

As I reflect now, January 2019, it has been eight years since I was there with Baba at the Samadhi. On the morning of my leaving, there were so many people around the Samadhi that I ended up behind the screen opposite the door, on a bench with the shoes. There was no way I had time to go in once more. As I looked through the screen wall, catching a blurry glimpse of the best place in the world, Baba clearly said, "We can never be separated," and I knew beyond any doubt that it was true.

"Go Back and Work!"

by Sahera Chohan

It was during my first visit in 2012, I was sitting on a wooden bench with a direct view into the Samadhi. Not many people were around—maybe one or two tidying up and sitting. I had not been doing a lot of work during that time of my life, I had been enjoying travelling and just hanging out....and I suddenly thought, "I could stay here and just hang out," when all of a sudden, it was as if Baba rose from His Tomb, pointed to me, and in no uncertain terms said quite directly and sternly, "Your place is in London—go back and work!"

I was taken aback—it was such a shock—I looked around to see if anyone else reacted, as it was as if Baba literally rose from His Tomb to instruct, command me. I "saw" Him, truly. But no one batted an eyelid. Since then, I did what Beloved Baba said, and have been working hard ever since. He taught me that it was time for me to take full financial responsibility for myself, be responsible and work. Jai Baba!

The Fragrance of Devotion

by Susan McKendree

One of the many lovely aspects of visiting Meher Baba's Samadhi is the opportunity to witness the acts of devotion made by other pilgrims. One of my most unforgettable memories is of sitting outside early one quiet afternoon when a young Indian couple arrived. The husband was dressed in the ubiquitous young man's attire of white shirt and black trousers. His tiny wife was wearing what was likely her best sari of freshly washed, faded orange cotton. They gave the appearance of being very poor. But it was what the young woman was holding in her arms that drew my eye: a tiny, obviously newborn infant, who, despite the heat, was bundled into a heavy orange blanket, and who was about to meet Baba for the very first time. The father went inside first, and when he came out the mother stepped in and carried the baby to Baba's feet. After bowing down herself she slowly turned the baby in her arms and bent down to touch its forehead to the cool marble. Then she stood and backed away.

I've heard many stories of how parents bring their newborns to lay them at Baba's feet, to surrender them to Him, of course, but perhaps also with the expectation of a blessing. However this baby's introduction to Meher Baba, so tenderly and lovingly performed, was to me the ultimate act of devotion: surrender, with no expectation of reward, only Love.

One morning when I was sitting inside, at the very front of the Samadhi, I heard someone step in and march—yes, march—up to Baba's Tomb. It was an elderly gentleman wearing a white Nehru jacket and hat. I know we're not meant to watch other lovers take darshan; however, I couldn't help but see him. As he stepped up to the Tomb, he clicked his heels and saluted the painting of Baba that hangs on the back wall. He then bowed down with military precision, touching his forehead to Baba's feet. After he arose, he clicked his heels again, saluted, and marched backward to the door, having paid obeisance to his Divine Commander-in-Chief.

But my most powerful memory is of visiting the Samadhi the day after Amartithi ended. We couldn't go inside yet. The bais were still cleaning, splashing buckets of water across the floor outside. But nothing could wash away the fragrance of devotion left behind by the thousands who had bowed down. As I breathed in the scent of wet stone and a lingering trace of flowers, I could feel soft waves of Baba's Love flowing out of the Samadhi. The very air beneath the pandal was hazy with it: it was palpable and visible to the eye. For three days the veil had been rent. I wanted to stay there forever.

The Well at World's End

by Max Reif

I've been to India and Meher Baba's Samadhi six times, the first in 1978. Most of the experiences blend and merge. The coming, the bowing and giving all of myself, or trying to, the repeated visits to soak up as much as I can, the holding onto the wall of the building while waiting in line... and the many many joys over the years, playing and listening to music in the hallowed antechamber... some of the best times of my life! One day in August, 2016, though, I had something of an "experience," and afterward tried to record its essence in this poem. AVATAR MEHER BABA KI JAI!

The Well at World's End   by Max Reif
Meherabad, August 16, 2016

Long ago, thirsty,
I went looking
for a well.
I searched
a lot of places,

until one day
I came upon
a small building
atop a modest hill—
a building the size of
a little room, really,
at the other end
of the world.

Inside the building
was a Well. Not
an ordinary well,
but a Well
of infinite depth;
and the thirst

its waters quenched
was not
a physical thirst.
How did I
ever come
to such a place?
I can't even say.

Oh, I have my story;
but you know,
that's only surface
blah-blah.

I don't see how anyone
could earn the right
to be here,
no matter how
much good he or she
has done.

For you see,
this Well
is brimming over with
the Waters of Life—
the Elixir
all the world
is seeking.

This water
is not even wet
in the usual way,
yet as I sit there
and it bubbles up
incessantly from No-Place,

I find myself bathed
in something clear and bright
that is all Answer
and no questions.

There's a sense
of a Someone,
a Someone of pure Light,
a Someone that
everyone longs for.
Over time, though,
I realized this Someone
is also me—the real me,
in fact, the Self
of all selves.

What I had thought
was me
reveals itself
as a faint shadow.
No wonder
it never
felt secure!

When I sit
before the Well
in this small
building on
the hill

and the bright
waters bubble up,
I know
I am safe
and well.
This Pure Light
brooks no conflict,

and it need not think,
for it IS.

Sitting at the Well,
I know
that the world
will be also saved,
for this Love
dissolves all confusion,
hate and fear.
And slowly
It is making
itself known.

I have no doubt
about any of this.
Love inspires
absolute conviction.

My only dilemma
is that whenever
I leave here,
I begin to turn
into my old self again,
and that won't do
any more.

And so, I
am wondering
how long
I have to stay
before I can leave

this Well of wells,
knowing securely
that a portal
to these Waters
lives inside me!

This Light alone
can guide my soul,
for it is
the Soul of souls.

Events at the Samadhi

by Richard Budd

1. Tomb Cleaning

Every time I'm at Meherabad I like to get up early and go to the Samadhi to be there when the Tomb opens. There's something very special about taking in the strong, heady scent of the roses built up overnight when the doors open and the roses, etc., are carried out, leaving a trail of scent behind them.

Then we help with the process of clearing out the previous day's Tomb cloths, soiled overnight with the decaying mound of roses. Then there's the process of cleaning the Tomb of the dust and grime accumulated the previous day and night, each person there being allocated a particular task, supervised by Dolly or one of her associates before covering the Tomb with fresh cloths.

It almost feels as if you're helping get Baba washed and dressed, ready to receive the visitors that day.

It was on one such morning during the process of cleaning the Tomb that Marsha, my wife, who had been allocated a part of the Tomb to clean by Dolly, was inside.

Dolly came over to me from the Tomb and asked if Marsha was okay?

I said, "Yes, as far as I'm aware, why?"

"Well, she said, "she's behaving very strangely."

And just at that moment there was the most horrendous scream from the Tomb multiplied by the echo in the Tomb, which sent Dolly and the rest of us rushing to the Tomb, expecting rather the worst.

What we found was Marsha sitting laughing. When asked what had happened, she explained.

When she woke up that morning, she had the impression that Baba wanted her to be silent for the day. So instead of talking, she had been using gestures to converse, which explained why Dolly thought she was behaving strangely.

Everything had gone well until she was in the Tomb cleaning, immersed in what she was doing. She hadn't noticed a frog, camouflaged in a corner against the stonework. As she worked toward the corner it suddenly leaped up in front of her, and she involuntarily let out a scream, more from shock and surprise than anything else.

Marsha took it that Baba was having a great joke— having her believe she had to be silent and then surprising her with the frog.

A good laugh all round that morning!

2. A Light from Baba

One day when in the Samadhi I came out and was greeted by one of the Indian workers (I believe he is now in charge of aspects in running the Samadhi) carrying a ladder. He asked if I could help him by holding the ladder while he did some work in the Samadhi.

So we went back and he set the ladder up by the door inside the Samadhi, fortunately no one was about at the time requiring prayers. He returned a few minutes later with a large lamp which he handed to me and climbed the ladder. Curious, I looked to see what he was doing and saw that he was removing the large lamp from its holder above the door and was focused on lighting the Samadhi. I realised that in all the times I had come in and out of the Samadhi, I had never noticed where the light had come from, as my focus had been on Baba's Tomb and/or His picture, not on where the light came.

A little thought provoking from Baba, methinks.

He secured the new lamp and came down the ladder and we came out of the Samadhi. He thanked me for my help and was about to leave when I thought to ask, "How often does the light need changing?"

"Not very often, as they are very reliable, once maybe every ten years."

He asked if I would like to have the spent bulb. I thought about how long it had been in the Tomb and its energy, and said, "Please, and thank You, Baba."

3. More Toads

There is another story when I was staying at Meherabad from July to September just after the rains. Everything was lovely and green and we still had occasionally heavy showers. One day I was sitting on the bench at the rear looking into the Samadhi, when I noticed a toad coming out of the drainpipe at the right side of the Samadhi in front of Mani's grave. It started moving slowly towards the center of the Samadhi, and as it did so it was followed by another and then another, until there was a stream of them exiting the drainpipe. I have to admit that I was quite fascinated at the sight and wondered how they all managed to survive in there.

As the first toad neared the center, it was noticed by a pilgrim who tried to shoo it back out of the Samadhi, but only succeeded in making it change direction slightly to head straight to the Tomb. In the meantime, there was now a column of toads unloading from the drain and spreading in all directions across the Samadhi entrance. Several people by now were trying to shoo toads away from the Samadhi, but only succeeded in spreading them further around the Samadhi, until all that could be seen were pilgrims shooing toads in all directions, trying to prevent them from going into the Tomb. The more they tried the less successful they were, and I could only imagine Baba rolling about laughing at pilgrims chasing toads around the entrance of the Samadhi.

Eventually, the toads were evacuated from the Samadhi and normality was resumed, but it was very hard not to laugh during all of this.

4. Monsoon Downpour

One night in August 2017 at arti after prayers and during singing praises to Baba, I decided to sing one of Billy Connelly's songs—"if it wasn't for yer wellies, where wid you be?" Obviously I had to explain a few things—that wellies were Wellington boots etc., and then I got folks to sing the chorus a couple of times before fitting in the verses. Everyone seemed to enjoy and join in with the humour of the song.

We all then headed back to the new Meher Pilgrim Retreat for dinner and just as we got there the heavens opened and we had a monsoon downpour which lasted all night.

We woke to find the area around the Retreat completely flooded. Turned out the storm was out of season and exceptionally heavy, but very welcome. Meherabad was suffering from several years of drought and that year the rains had again been poor. Residents and locals were hoping that they might get sufficient rainfall in the later period of the monsoon. I was informed later that the rain that fell after singing at the Samadhi was sufficient to fill the wells and brought much relief to the area.

I was then being joked about for the rest of the trip as a rainmaker and told not to sing that song at the Samadhi except at the dry season.

Spring Cleaning

by Mehernoush McPherson

There are some waves of concerns circulating around lovers of Beloved Meher Baba about the current corona-virus outbreak, and they are wondering what dearest Baba is doing to the world! That inspired me to share a vision of Beloved Baba that I had in His Samadhi on my recent visit to Meherabad in early February of 2020.

Like many of you who have had visions of Meher Baba, I am sure it was not of my own imagination. Since, when Baba appears to you in a vision, He comes with all His attributes, affection and His Divine Character. The visions of Beloved Baba are so vivid that even the colors are brighter, the atmosphere becomes more joyful and the whole world disappears from your sight and you only see Him and what He wants you to see.

The visions of Beloved Baba always have a message within them and it comes directly and clearly from Him. We as His lovers usually prefer not to share those visions, since we feel they are so intimate to us and they are not meant to be told. But this time I feel strongly that Dearest Baba wants me to share this vision of Him with His Lovers—perhaps since it does concern us all.

It was either the 5th, 6th or the 7th of February 2020, (sorry, I didn't write down the date) just before my return to America. I was at the Samadhi and it was just before the start of the evening arti and people were gathering to perform the arti. I was sitting on the area rug which had been spread in front of entrance door to the Samadhi. There were a few ladies, Indians, Persians, Asians and Westerners, sitting next to and in front of me and we were all focused on Baba.

Then suddenly, I saw Beloved Baba appear in the Samadhi, standing just right of where people bow down to His Tombstone, facing us. He was wearing His blue coat on top of His long sadra. His hair was tied in the back. Baba looked serious and was silent. As He appeared, everything in the Samadhi became more colorful! The flowers became all bright pink and there was a spectrum of beautiful blue, purple and violet colors—it seemed that the sun was shining through them!

Beloved Baba appeared to be a little anxious. It was like He was going to do something big. He wasn't looking at me nor He was smiling! Next to Baba on His left side there was a commercial vacuum cleaner by His feet on the floor. Its color was white and it was big! Beloved Baba was holding the air tube of the vacuum, which was attached to the duct hose with His left hand. His right hand was in His pocket, and I felt that at any moment Baba was going to take His right hand out of His pocket and turn the switch on and start the vacuum!

Seeing this, I told Baba inwardly, "Yes, Baba dear, see how sinful I have become—that now you have to bring a heavy-duty vacuum to clean my sanskaras from me! Then I thought perhaps Baba is going to clean all of His lovers who have gathered here! (Usually Baba washed and cleaned His lovers with a sponge, or used a tumbler filled with water and a soap. Seeing Baba with a commercial vacuum cleaner seemed somewhat harsh). Yet, I told Baba, " Here I am, here we are, ready to be cleaned, Baba, by You—whatever it takes."

Then suddenly I felt someone had lifted me off the ground and I was about a hundred feet above the dome of the Samadhi looking down. Even the dome and the whole Samadhi and the trees from above looked so heavenly colorful! Then I realized that I could see the big picture! I saw tunnels of wind all in high speed, leading to Baba's Samadhi, flying through all three windows and the door, bringing with them garbage, rubbish, dirt and impurities into the Samadhi! I knew then that Baba had just turned on the heavy-duty vacuum and had just started vacuuming the whole world from all directions, taking all the impurities to Himself, to His Samadhi. Cleaning!

I thought, "Wow! This is huge! Baba is doing a Universal Cleaning!" Then I was back, sitting among the others on that area rug!

Now every time that I think of this powerful vision of Baba, it reminds me of the spring cleaning that is customary among Iranians worldwide before Nowruz, the Persian New Year! Perhaps Baba started an early spring cleaning and now the whole world was participating in it by cleaning and sanitizing! I hope that since Baba turned on the vacuum and things accelerated, He will also turn off the switch so things will slow down!

I have heard that since the corona-virus outbreak, the carbon monoxide emissions have decreased by more than 25% in the world, and the oceans and rivers are less polluted now. The dolphins are coming back to Venice, the bulls are safe in Spain, people have stopped eating bats in China and army troops, instead of being sent out to fight wars, are being sent out to save lives! Yes, Mother Nature needed to get a nice sponge bath and who could have done such a great job, except The Avatar!

Jai Meher Baba!

How Much Baba Loves Us

by Anonymous

When I go to the Samadhi I try to focus on how much I love Baba and hope to do so more and more, yet I find it hard to feel worthy of the love He feels for every individual one of us. But at times when I am receptive I hear His voice—the gentlest, softest stillest voice, full of love asking: "Please don't go yet. Can't you wait just a little bit more?" However much we love Him, He loves us infinitely more.

CPSIA information can be obtained
at www.ICGtesting.com
Printed in the USA
LVHW091052261020
669836LV00006B/114

9 780578 760407